When You Walk Through the Fire

The Bethany Rivas Story

by Sharon Rivas

God bless,

Sharon Rivas

4/29/18

FarMor
Group
Inc.
*Formed in
God's Image*

Orlando, FL

When You Walk Through the Fire:
The Bethany Rivas Story
Copyright © 2014 by Sharon Rivas

ISBN 13: 978-0-9911974-0-8
ISBN 10: 0-9911974-0-2

Published by:
FarMor Publishing Company
A division of FarMor Group Inc.
P.O. Box 585633
Orlando, FL 32858
www.farmorgroupinc.com

Cover image by Kate Johnson (kjphotographyfl.com)
Author photo on back cover by Avis-Marie Barnes

Printed in the United States

Library of Congress Control Number: 2013955386

Dedication

This book is dedicated to the One
whose peace surpasses all understanding,
who gives calm in the midst of a storm and
who comforts and strengthens me daily.
I can say from experience, that if we let Him, God's love
and forgiveness can turn a tragedy into a testimony.

*"He heals the brokenhearted and binds up
their wounds."* (Psalm 147:3, NIV)

Acknowledgments

My deepest gratitude and appreciation go out to the following people:

Suzette Farquharson-Morgan for making it possible to do what so many others had encouraged me to do. Thank you for contacting me, for standing by us during the trial and for giving me help, advice and support during the writing and publishing of this book.

My family for being patient with me while I was writing: to **Clark** for cooking and putting up with all the clutter; to **Clint** for sharing his mother with a computer; and to **Kristin** for refreshing my memories on certain events, such as reassuring me the "hermit crab incident" really *did* take place...no matter how absurd it sounds.

Pastor Rick Page and Faith Family Community Church, the Rivas and Folsom families, and the 300 friends who attended Bethany's funeral for your constant love and support, and for giving us food, flowers and funds to help us through the tragedy.

Kim Nichols for calling me immediately after hearing my testimony about Bethany's death and telling me I needed to share it with others...and for giving me the opportunity to do so at the next ladies retreat.

Kevin and Candy Fischer for the bond our shared loss has created. Somehow crying together, standing beside each other at our daughters' graves and supporting one another during the trial gave us *all* a little more strength.

Donna Weinheimer for being willing to help answer my prayer the night Bethany died, and for her friendship afterward.

Pastor Zachery Tims, Jr. for the messages that gave me strength to get out of bed in the months after Bethany died, and for his words of encouragement at Borders bookstore that motivated me to keep writing.

Ann Adams and Yolanda Larson for inviting me to join MADD and share my story. It was seeing the way it impacted others that made me realize the importance of writing this book.

Jeff Welch at West Orlando Custom Build for the laptop that has been my constant companion and for his assistance with any computer needs I had thereafter.

My fellow co-workers for their constant encouragement and support, especially: **Tony Newton** for encouraging me to write a chapter each day and for proofreading and offering literary suggestions; **Paul Cloud** for creating the original memorial booklet site on blogspot.com; **Alex Krawtschenko** for hosting her former website at RememberBethany.com; **Kethleen Holthausen** for translating the booklet into Portuguese; and to **Auriellelhy Benacourt** for translating the booklet into Spanish (www.bethanyrivas-es.blogspot.com).

Table of Contents

"When you pass through the waters, I will be with you; and through the rivers, they shall not overflow you. **When you walk through the fire,** *you shall not be burned, nor shall the flame scorch you."*

— Isaiah 43:2 (NKJV)

Chapter 1:

Facing Death

It was January 12, 2011. The night was pitch-black, and the road was wet and winding. I had gotten off work late and noticed it was almost 11 p.m. as I headed home.

I was taking a two-lane, backwoods road that was known for its sharp curves and lack of streetlights. It had rained earlier, so a heavy mist hung in the air, which made the road even more treacherous.

After a few miles, a sports car flew pass me and several other cars that were driving cautiously. I cringed as his taillights disappeared into the fog ahead.

"What an idiot!" I said out loud.

Then with deepening apprehension I thought, "He's going to lose control of that car on this slick road and wrap it around a tree.

"He doesn't realize how quickly life can end. One minute you're alive, and the next minute you're dead, with no time for good-byes."

Immediately, a familiar pain pierced my heart.

The memory of my daughter's death always lingered in the back of my mind, but tonight it was especially strong.

It had been on a dark, winding, backwoods road—similar to this one—that my 19-year-old daughter, Bethany, had lost her life.

On March 6, 2005, she had left a birthday party with three others in the car.

Around 11 p.m., the driver lost control going around a curve and slammed into an electric pole, killing Bethany and her friend, Crystal Fischer.

For the past six years, I had wondered about those final moments:

Did my daughter know she was going to die? Was she afraid? Did she have time to think or pray? Were her last thoughts of her family and how devastated we would be?

I was contemplating these things as I rounded the last curve.

Suddenly, my back tires slid off the pavement and into the loose gravel on the side of the road. I had no traction and was sliding toward a metal signpost.

Instantly, I yanked the wheel to the left, fighting to get the car back onto the road and avoid the pole. I missed it by inches, but then my car careened out of control and swerved into the other lane.

I slammed on the brake and fought to regain control, but it was no use. My Kia Spectra began to spin, and I was instantly hydroplaning into oncoming traffic.

I quickly realized that the person coming toward me would have no time to brake and avoid hitting me.

We were both going too fast, and there were only a few feet between us.

I also noticed a large, electric pole, which I was heading directly for as I slid across the road.

Although it had taken only seconds to lose control of my car, time seemed to pass in slow motion. Perhaps the rush of adrenalin heightens our senses in a crisis.

I had ample time to realize I was *facing death* and to actually process the irony that I was going to die in nearly the same manner my daughter did—in a similar location—at the same time. I was able to think sharp, concise concepts, instantaneously.

I took inventory of my life. Was I ready to meet God? Yes! Was the driver in the other car going to die tonight? Possibly.

Already I felt remorse that I may kill or injure an innocent person, but I was helpless.

Then a strange thing happened. Although I had no time to organize my thoughts into a prayer, I *heard* myself cry, "God help me!"

I did not have time to think in full sentences, but my soul had time to call out to its Maker. I realized I was not asking for deliverance, because I saw no possible way of escape, but I was asking for strength to die well.

And then, the last thought that crossed my mind was of my family losing me so soon after burying Bethany. I was devastated that I could not tell them good-bye.

As my car spun, it turned just enough to miss the oncoming car by inches. But I quickly saw I was still destined to slam into the looming light pole.

Suddenly, the car skidded to a stop. I sat in stunned silence as I stared at the pole, not more than 10 or 12 inches in front of my bumper.

Along both sides of the road, drivers pulled over, got out of their cars and peered at me through the darkness.

They were probably as shocked as I was to see me alive and my car in one piece, without any scratches or dents.

My heart was pounding and I was shaken to the core, but I knew instantly that I had experienced divine protection.

"Thank You, God," I said aloud.

Noticing the 12-inch space between my bumper and the pole (as though someone had guided my car to a sudden stop), I whispered, "Thanks, Bethany," just in case she'd been my guardian angel that night.

I would soon discover my premonition was right.

For several minutes I sat limp—drained of energy. Then I slowly backed up and pulled onto the road, making a U-turn to head in the right direction.

As I drove home, I realized I had been allowed a unique opportunity. I had faced death and lived.

Now, I also knew what might have gone through my daughter's mind. She *could have reviewed her life in an instant*, called out to God and longed to tell us good-bye in her dying thoughts.

Could it be I was allowed this near-death experience so I would know what Bethany had gone through? Or, was it merely a coincidence and she had been there to protect me?

I could almost hear her saying, "I've got your back, Mom! It wasn't your time to die tonight."

Then with a twinkle in her eyes, adding, "And you need to slow down on wet roads, too—and don't be so quick to criticize next time!"

A few days later, I met Kathy, a co-worker of mine, for lunch. We exchanged Christmas gifts at the restaurant, since we hadn't gotten a chance over the holidays.

As she handed me the gift, Kathy said, "I hope this doesn't make you cry. I had planned to give you something else, but it seemed like I was supposed to give this to you."

Inside the gift bag was a gold devotional book called *Angels Everywhere*, which is full of true stories from people who had experienced something they could only attribute to a guardian angel.

There was also a beautiful figurine of an angel looking over a kneeling woman. The inscription read, "Laugh and cry for the ones gone, for they send angels to watch over you until you see them again."

Delighted, I immediately explained how appropriate the words were on it. I shared the near catastrophe and how I escaped, as if "someone" had protected me.

Kathy quickly responded, "Then it must have been Bethany telling me to get this gift. I felt so compelled to buy the angel for you, and now I know why.

"She knew what was going to happen and wanted you to know she was there for you!"

A couple weeks later, I picked up the devotional Kathy gave me. I intended to start at the beginning but when I opened the book, it randomly went to a story in the middle titled, "THE ACCIDENT THAT NEVER WAS."[1]

To my amazement, the story was about an incident that occurred on a dark, rainy night in which a man had miraculously escaped a horrible collision.

The driver was sitting at a red light when he noticed in his rear-view mirror that the vehicle behind him was swerving out of control toward his car.

Realizing there was no way to escape the hit, he prayed "Please, God, help me."

Suddenly, his car was lifted up. He heard vehicles slamming into each other but never felt the impact himself.

When everyone came over to see the damage, they asked him if he was hurt. The man told them that he had not been in the collision.

They immediately wanted to know *how* that was possible, since they had all seen his car move through the air and land on the median.

Upon examining his car, they were amazed to discover it did not have a scratch on it. The driver concluded that a guardian angel had, indeed, answered his prayer.

Tears ran down my cheeks as I read the story. I knew it was not a coincidence that I had "randomly" opened the book to this particular page.

It was another divine message from beyond, just as I had experienced the night Bethany died.

Sandwiches

It was 9:30 p.m. on Sunday, March 6, 2005. I remember that night well. I was standing alone in the kitchen, making stacks of sandwiches and wondering why.

It was an unusual evening because everyone else had gone to bed early. Usually, my husband stayed up late, but Clark was extremely tired so he went to bed.

Our son, Clint, who was in the 6th grade, had a week-long state test starting that week, so he needed plenty of rest.

Kristin, our 17-year-old daughter, was also asleep because she had to leave at 6 a.m. to be back at Southeastern University in Lakeland, Florida.

She had graduated from West Orange High School in Winter Garden, a year early, alongside her sister, Bethany. Now she was a freshman in the university's missions program.

Before going to bed, Kristin had shared the unusual events which occurred during church service that evening.

The guest speaker was Dr. Mike Rakes, the vice president of her college. He had invited anyone who wanted healing to come forward.

Since Kristin had not been feeling well, she went to the altar. When he laid hands on her and prayed, her sore throat went away.

However, Dr. Rakes said he also felt led to pray that God would give her the strength and courage she needed to get through a crisis in her life.

She wondered, "What crisis?" I also contemplated that question as I made the sandwiches.

Everything seemed to be going just fine in our lives. Kristin and her boyfriend of three years were enrolled in the same missions program.

Our 19-year-old daughter, Bethany, had moved in with her boyfriend, Justin, when she turned 18.

We had welcomed the young men into our family and loved them both.

My only disappointment was that Bethany had recently detoured from our family's roots of traditional faith and was no longer attending church.

My husband and I were raised in Christian homes and all of our relatives, from generations back, had been active in ministry. Clark had also been a pastor for 10 years.

His grandfather, Clinton Calhoun (for whom our son was named), and my grandfather, William Folsom, were pastors and had planted several churches.

I grew up hearing my mother and her younger sister, Margaret, tell exciting tales from Africa and Central America where they had been missionaries. They were proud of Kristin for wanting to follow in their footsteps.

However, I believed in my heart that Bethany would return to God *someday*, perhaps after she was married and had children.

I continued to pray for her and Justin faithfully every morning at 5:30 during my devotions.

As I made the sandwiches and zipped them in baggies, I couldn't help but wonder what sudden urge had possessed me to make lunch for my family.

I had never done this before. Clint had always bought school lunch, and Clark, who was driving a commercial truck at the time, normally went to a drive-thru.

It may have been because we were a little tight on money. Whatever the reason, instead of just making a couple of sandwiches for the next day, I used two loaves of bread to make peanut butter, turkey and tuna fish sandwiches.

This fact may not seem important, but I assure you, I was absolutely dead tired and wanted to sleep. Yet, I still felt "compelled" to keep making them.

I discovered why…the next day.

Chapter 2:

God Speaks

After finishing the sandwiches, I trudged wearily upstairs and dropped into bed. It was 10 p.m. and I set my alarm for 5:30 a.m.

As always, I rolled over on my side and snuggled down into my pillow. I was just dosing off peacefully when I heard, *"Pray for Bethany!"* The thought was not my own.

I had experienced this before and knew it was God. Normally, I tried hard to obey, but this time, I actually argued with Him.

"Lord, I'm so tired. Can't I pray for her at 5:30 like I normally do every morning?"

Once more, I drifted off to sleep.

"ROLL OVER ON YOUR BACK!" This time the thought was even more urgent, and I sensed God wanted me to stay awake and listen.

That happens sometimes. I can actually feel the emotion behind the thought. I can tell if He is smiling or disappointed in me.

It is more than just hearing it in the tone of His voice. Even when He chides me, there is always the underlying sense of unconditional love.

Very rarely have I heard actual words. Most of the time, it is a thought so different from my own that I know it is coming from an "outside" source.

People often ask me how I know it is God talking and not just my own thoughts.

I tell them, "If you honestly don't know the solution to a problem or situation and you ask God, and if the answer comes almost immediately (and it surprises or even upsets you), then it is obviously not something you told yourself."

That's what happened at 10 p.m. on Sunday, March 6, 2005, when God told me to wake up and pray for Bethany. He stressed *it couldn't wait until morning.*

When I asked why, the answer greatly upset me.

God said, "You've been praying two years for Bethany to return to her faith and for her protection while she was away from Me. Tonight I need you to change your prayer.

"I want you to *release her soul* to Me. I need to know if you are willing to pray that I will do *whatever* it takes to bring her back to Me, including suffering and death."

Now, I love the Lord very much but, immediately, I said "NO!" What mother would agree to let her child suffer and die in order to come back to Him? I wanted God to save her soul…*and her life!*

Although He didn't seem angry when I refused, I quickly realized that He was *asking*…allowing me free will to make the decision myself.

I could keep saying no, but I could sense the dire consequences of my actions. God was waiting patiently for me to willingly let go.

Looking back, I should have known something would happen to Bethany that night because He said *I could not wait until morning to pray for her.*

Even then, I did not put together the other clues He had given me recently. That would come a few hours later…on the way to the hospital.

I began to plead with God and even begged Him to take my life instead.

Again He asked, "Are you willing for Me to do WHATEVER it takes to bring Bethany back to Me?"

I realized I had to make a decision. Would I rather have Bethany with me on earth for a short time and risk her going into eternity lost?

Or, would I rather have her go to heaven and know that we will be together forever?

The choice was obvious but an excruciating one. I wanted Bethany to be with us in heaven, but I could not face spending years here on earth without her.

The emotional pain was severe. I buried my head in the pillow to muffle the sound of my sobs.

I cried so hard and so long that the pillowcase was soaked and my head was throbbing.

I wept until I literally had no tears left. Finally, I came to terms with the love I had for Bethany, *as my child*, and my love for *her soul*.

It was a gut-wrenching moment, but I knew I had to let go and do what was best for her, not me. Her soul was more important.

I made God promise that if I released her soul to Him, He would send someone *to hold her and pray with her till her last breath*. I asked several times.

The only way I could deal with my daughter's death was if God let me know He would give her every possible chance to get right with Him, down to her last breath.

I envisioned her on a stretcher in the hospital and a nurse holding her hand and praying with her.

Suddenly, I felt peace that God would grant my request.

When I finally looked at the clock it was almost 11 p.m. I had agonized over my decision for one hour.

Exhausted, I rolled back on my side and fell asleep... not knowing that Bethany would die *that night*.

3 a.m.

I had often heard that 3 a.m. was when evil things happen to people. It's called the "witching hour" because it is the opposite of 3 p.m., when Christ died on the cross.

There were many TV documentaries about tragedies occurring at this hour, but I never thought it would happen to me.

After only a few hours sleep, I awoke to the sound of the telephone ringing in the kitchen.

The phone in the bedroom was unplugged, so I was surprised I heard the one downstairs ringing. I stayed in bed listening but did not open my eyes. I hoped it was a wrong number.

When it immediately began ringing again, a strange fear rose inside me.

I could hear a male voice leaving a message on the answering machine. It was too faint to understand, but it sounded urgent.

Clark was still sleeping so I did not wake him.

Reluctant to face the cold, I forced myself out of bed and wrapped a robe around me. I clung to the banister as I felt my way downstairs in the dark.

With each step, I tried to quell the churning in my stomach. I could not face the possibility that the message might be about Bethany.

Instead, I wondered if it was my Uncle David calling to tell me that my mother had passed away.

She was in her 80s and had become very frail...but, in my gut, there was a gnawing fear that this call was about my daughter.

My hand trembled as I pressed the play button on the answering machine and held my breath.

As I listened to the message, waves of nausea swept over me. It was a man from Orlando Regional Medical Center looking for the parents of Bethany Rivas. He needed us to call him immediately.

My heart pounded as I dialed the number. When he answered, I told him I was Bethany's mother.

"Ma'am, your daughter has just been in a terrible car accident. We need you to come to the emergency room right away!"

"Is she okay?" I asked anxiously. "Is she conscious?"

"I can't discuss her condition over the phone, Mrs. Rivas. You'll have to come to the emergency room."

"What about her boyfriend?" I asked. "Is he there? Is he conscious?"

"You mean Justin? Yes, he's here. They were in the accident together. He's injured but conscious."

I thought it was strange that when I asked if Justin was conscious, the gentleman responded — without hesitation.

Again, I asked if he could tell me anything about Bethany.

He hesitated, and then spoke softly that her condition was serious, but he could not give me any details over the phone. My husband and I would have to come to the hospital so he could talk to us *in person*.

It was then that my insides turned to liquid and drained to the bottom of my feet. I knew in my gut she was dead.

I began shivering and perspiring with cold chills. God had just told me Bethany was going to die...*but so soon?*

I turned and looked at the clock. It was *exactly* 3 a.m.

Chapter 3:

My Turn

My legs felt like Jell-O as I climbed the stairs. Now I understood that God had been preparing me for Bethany's death. However, I could not discuss this with my husband.

I woke Clark up and told him about the phone call but not about my conversation with God.

After quickly getting dressed, I taped a note on our children's bathroom mirror, explaining that their sister had been in an accident and we had gone to the emergency room.

Thinking Bethany might be going into surgery, Clark urged me to bring a book and pillow, just in case we would be there awhile. I did as he suggested but inwardly, I held out little hope.

We spent most of the 30-minute drive to the hospital in silence. It was an eerie time.

The highway, which was normally jammed with cars and noise, was empty and silent in the darkness.

I finally decided to prepare my husband for the worst.

As gently as possible I said, "Clark, the man refused to discuss Bethany's condition over the phone. She might be dead, Sweetheart."

Instantly he shot back, "NO! That's not *even* a possibility!" He said it so sternly and emphatically that I did not press the issue.

Instead, I made him promise that if she was alive, he would pray with her immediately, in case she didn't make it.

Clark remained quiet. I could tell he was scared but he was trying not to show it.

As we drove silently, I began to recall some of the strange omens that had taken place recently.

A few weeks before, I was taking a box of knickknacks to the thrift store, including some vases Bethany had given me over the years.

When I approached the car, a voice suddenly pierced my thoughts, "If something happens to Bethany, those won't be junk—they'll be treasure!"

The feeling was so strong that I actually stopped and walked back in the house. I put every item Bethany had given me on a shelf in my closet. Then I took the rest to Goodwill.

A few days later, Bethany left a voice message on my cell phone, inviting me to go shopping with her. After listening to it, I went to erase the message but *something* said not to.

I paused before hitting the delete button but told myself the feeling was silly and erased the message.

Several weeks later, *it* happened again.

Bethany had taken me to lunch on February 4 to celebrate my birthday. She surprised me by inviting Clark and her boyfriend, and loading the restaurant table with gifts.

On February 14, I felt compelled to send her a card, thanking her for everything she'd done and telling her how much I loved and missed her.

The next day when I got home from work, I saw the light blinking on the answering machine. It was Bethany in her bubbly voice, thanking me for the Valentine's Day card with the sweet message.

Then she added, "I miss you, too, Mom, and I love you very much. I can't wait to see you. Thanks again for the beautiful card!"

I started to press the delete button, but again the inner voice said, "If something happens to Bethany, you'll wish you had kept this message."

I was truly worried. This was the third time I had received the warning. In fact, it scared me enough that I hit the save button instead.

Every three days, the light would blink, indicating that I had a saved message. When the answering machine asked if I wanted to delete it, I kept the message three more times.

On the fourth time, I realized it had been 12 days and nothing had happened to Bethany. It had been a month since I rescued her vases out of the Goodwill box.

I told myself that I was developing a phobia, and the only way to overcome it was to face my fear and conquer it.

My insides were in turmoil but, with bold determination, I reached over and pressed the delete button.

Now, as Clark and I raced through the darkness to the hospital, I had a horrible feeling in the pit of my stomach.

The knickknacks she had given me were still on my closet shelf but her beautiful messages were gone.

I wanted to hold Bethany's hand one more time, brush her face with my fingers and kiss her, but I had a sinking feeling that it was too late.

When we arrived at the large, downtown hospital, the emergency room was brightly lit with people crammed wall to wall.

There was a lot of talking and a TV blaring. The young man and woman on night duty were actually giggling about something, while one spun around in a chair.

However, when Clark and I approached the desk and gave our names, the giggling and spinning ended abruptly.

They both turned pale. I realized then that my worst fears were about to come true.

The young man and woman looked at each other with an expression I will never forget. It read, *Oh my God, they're here. They're going to find out their daughter is **dead**!*

The young lady dialed an extension and whispered to someone with a strained voice that we had arrived. She hung up and said someone would be with us momentarily.

It was obvious that neither she nor her co-worker wanted to make eye contact with us.

Within seconds, a man dressed in a suit entered the waiting room and asked us to follow him. I was surprised, since I was expecting to see a doctor.

The gentleman explained that he was an administrator and escorted us to a small room where a female doctor in scrubs was waiting for us.

I could sense from their somber expressions that Clark and I were in for bad news.

All my life I had watched newscasts chronicling the tragedies of others: homicides; house fires; car accidents; deadly tornadoes....

I had also seen family members weeping over the death of their loved ones and thought, "Why have I been so *lucky*?"

I often prayed for families who had suffered a loss and asked God to give me strength and courage to face a tragedy, if one arose.

No matter what happened, I wanted the world to see that I believe God is in control and my faith would not waver.

As the administrator closed the door, I prayed, "God help me! This time, I think it's *my turn*."

Chapter 4:

Facing Reality

I don't know exactly how I imagined a doctor or police officer would tell you that your loved one is dead, but I definitely expected to see some emotion. I have learned the opposite is true.

The bearers of bad news steel themselves and try not to show their feelings because they know how traumatic the experience is.

I could hardly comprehend that Clark and I were being told our daughter was dead.

The female doctor calmly took my hand and assured me that they had tried to revive her for 30 minutes at the hospital but couldn't.

Apparently, Bethany had been at a party where she and her friends had been drinking. The doctor suspected that all four passengers in the car were under the influence when the accident occurred.

She said my daughter and another girl were killed instantly.

"It's sad that so many young people die in drunk-driving accidents," she added.

Then she and the administrator simply stared at us. Although they appeared sympathetic, breaking the news to us in such a calm, polite way made Bethany's death seem unreal.

I guess shock sets in immediately because I felt numb.

In fact, instead of sobbing or screaming uncontrollably, I became angry.

When I found out Bethany had been drinking and that she had died needlessly because of it, I was actually upset with her.

I looked at the doctor and the administrator and said, "You know, Bethany was raised in a Christian home. A year ago, she moved out because she said she wanted to try life for a while *without* God.

"I told her that was a very dangerous place to be—out from under the protection of God. And now she's dead!"

They both stared at me strangely. I guess they've seen people react many ways, but my response may have caught them off guard.

Looking back, it seems unbelievable that neither Clark nor I cried right away. I would have thought parents who had just been told their daughter was killed would have burst into tears.

Instead, we asked if we could go to the morgue. We needed to see her…to comprehend if this was real…to hold her in our arms and say good-bye.

However, they refused to let us go. They said we should remember her the way she was. Even though we insisted, they were adamant.

Since we could not see Bethany, we asked to see her boyfriend. This time the doctor agreed.

Justin was in ICU with serious injuries. Though conscious, he was very groggy and in a lot of pain.

We held his hand, and Clark prayed for his recovery as well as strength for all of us. We then broke the news that Bethany was dead.

Justin was so sedated, he simply stared at us and nodded.

After we were ushered out his room, Clark and I walked down the hall alone.

Since it was still night, only dim lights were on and everything was quiet.

I kept looking down at my feet, just trying to put one foot in front of the other.

It was then that I realized the doctor had said Bethany died "instantly" and they were unable to revive her.

My heart was crushed with overwhelming doubt and despair. Not only did we lose our daughter, which was unbearable, but it seemed like God had not kept His promise.

I cried out to Him to give me strength and faith. As I stared at the floor, part of a Bible verse I had learned as a child came back to me and resounded in my head.

Yea, though I walk through the valley of the shadow of death...thou art with me... (Psalm 23:4, KJV). I repeated these words with each step I took.

Slowly, a peace that surpasses all understanding began to calm the storm inside me.

As Clark and I stepped out of the hospital doors, we saw a reporter filming a newscast about the accident.

We stood quietly nearby, listening to details the doctor had not given us. It was then that we learned our daughter had been ejected from the car.

When the reporter finished and the camera was turned off, we stepped forward and introduced ourselves as Bethany's parents.

The young lady offered her condolences and asked if we would like to say anything to warn other teenagers about the dangers of drunk driving. We agreed.

"Bethany had her whole life ahead of her," I said. "And now because she was in the car with someone who was drinking and driving, we just had to tell her boyfriend that the girl he loved and was going to marry is dead!"

After the interview, Clark and I walked slowly to the parking lot. The shock finally wore off and our tears burst forth like a dam as we both sobbed uncontrollably.

It was almost 5 a.m., and Clark was supposed to be at work by 6 a.m. When he called and told his boss the news, there was a long pause.

Once the shock wore off, Skip offered his condolences and told Clark to take all the time he needed.

The kindness and concern shown from the company touched us deeply, especially since my husband had just started working there two weeks before.

As we sat in the car, we decided to call Justin's mom since we did not see her at the hospital. We figured Donna and her husband, Randy, would be getting ready for work.

Apparently, they had not known anything about the accident. When I told her Justin was in the emergency room, she screamed for Randy and hung up.

We knew she would have enough pain finding out about her own son—no need to tell her that the girl she loved like a daughter was already dead.

The following hours were a blur. By then, I was hysterical with grief and do not recall the drive home.

The next thing I do remember is seeing the neighbors' bedroom light on when we pulled into our driveway and thinking, "I should call Dave and Trish right away."

Bethany had often babysat their 8-year-old daughter, Brianna, and the couple was expecting another child in a few weeks. I had been eager to see how Bethany would handle taking care of a baby.

I was also looking forward to the day when she got married and started a family. I used to fear getting old but realized I was already anticipating being a grandmother.

Now, it was impossible to fathom that I would never hold my daughter again and that she would never hold a baby of her own. Finally, I mustered up the courage to call.

I will never forget the gasp of disbelief as I told Trish the news or the sound of her voice shouting to David that Bethany had been killed.

This was only the beginning of the calls we had to make. Clark and I made a list and had the painful task of deciding which one of us would phone various family and friends.

As we reviewed the list, the 6 a.m. news came on. The story of the terrible crash in Groveland leaving two dead and two critically injured led the newscast.

I watched the taped interview I had given earlier that morning. Within minutes, the pastor of Kristin's church, which we had also attended for several years, called to pray with us over the phone.

After Pastor Basil's call, we continued phoning others.

The most difficult thing we had to do was tell our children who were still asleep upstairs. We wanted them to rest as long as possible since we knew they would face many exhausting days ahead.

At 6:30 a.m., Clark woke Kristin and Clint up so we could tell them about their sister in private before people started arriving at the house.

It is too painful to describe those awful moments with our children that morning. Telling them about the accident and seeing them break down and sob was gut-wrenching.

Even worse was the thought that Bethany might have gone into eternity lost and we would never see her again.

We all held each other and wept openly. It felt like a nightmare, but the ringing phones and doorbell assured us it was real. Those calls and visits kept us from caving completely into despair.

Immediately, loved ones from all over the city, including those we had not seen in years, began pouring into our home to comfort us. Their love and support was crucial to our emotional survival those first few days.

When you are in shock from the loss of a loved one, you often lose your appetite and feel completely drained of energy. Usually, all you want to do is sleep to escape the nightmare of reality, but sleep eludes you.

The pain and fear keep you awake, and at times it is hard to think rationally. So when others step in and help you, it is a true gift.

Pat, one of my closest friends from church, arrived with cleaning supplies. Other friends from all over the city began bringing food.

Esther, who was in bed sick, sent her husband over with a huge basket full of paper plates, cups, plastic silverware, paper towels and toilet paper.

Those were some of the most practical things we received. In fact, there were so many tears shed that we finished every box of Kleenex, every roll of toilet paper and all the paper towels in the house.

Our visitors also went through the piles of sandwiches I had felt compelled to make the night before. Even in something as small as this, God had prepared us.

Gradually, we began to find out more information about the accident through the news and police reports. We learned the name of the other victim was Crystal Fischer.

Bethany and Crystal had gone to the Central Florida Fair on Saturday night with a group of friends. Then they spent the night at a friend's home to help prepare for a birthday party the next day.

During the party, Crystal, Bethany and her boyfriend volunteered to go to the store. Because Justin had been drinking, he did not want to drive.

Steven, an older guy who was a friend of the homeowner, offered to take them in Justin's car. Since he, too, had been drinking, friends warned them not to go. However, the pleas fell on deaf ears.

Several miles down the road on an "S" curve, the two-door Kia Spectra they were in spun out of control and hit a light pole, breaking it in two before slamming into a tree.

Crystal was killed instantly, and Bethany was ejected through the rear windshield.

Steven had a concussion, and Justin was badly injured. Both were rushed to the hospital.

Although the details of the accident were unpleasant, our families were glad to know Bethany and Crystal had been friends. Our common grief soon created a strong bond, especially between me and Crystal's mother, Candy.

Many times, day or night, we would call each other for support. This support proved invaluable, 10 months later, when each family faced another unexpected crisis.

Candy Fischer with her daughters, Lora Ann (left) and Crystal (right).

Later Monday morning, our pastor, Rick Page, came over with his wife, Lora.

It was then that I related the entire story of what had happened the night before when God spoke to me.

I confided in my pastor that I had asked God to send someone to pray with Bethany. I felt sure He had promised me He would, only to hear that she was killed instantly.

Pastor Rick assured me there are some things we cannot understand. But we know, as it says in Genesis 18:25, that God will do what is right.

He and his wife spent most of the day with us and gave us tremendous support.

Since Clark and I were told we should not see Bethany, it was Pastor Rick and Lora who agreed to go to the coroner's office to identify her.

We are grateful to them for helping us in such a special way. As much as I wanted to see Bethany, I don't believe I could have handled it at the time.

I'm sure it would have been extremely painful and may have left emotional scars.

While Clark was on the phone with the coroner's office, making arrangements for our pastor to identify her body, he received some startling news.

The coroner informed my husband that a lady at the scene of the accident had performed CPR on Bethany.

He said he was amazed to note that, even though Bethany had broken almost every bone in her body, she had been revived and actually lived a few minutes longer.

After Clark told me the news, my heart leapt with hope!

When Pastor Rick and his wife returned that afternoon, I told them what happened.

"God did not fail me!" I exclaimed. "He sent someone to resuscitate Bethany and give her the opportunity to make peace with Him."

Although we tried to get information from the police about the woman, they would not give us any details. Since it was a vehicular homicide case, she was considered a witness and we were not allowed to contact her.

I was deeply disappointed and wondered if I would ever find out who she was and, more importantly, if she had prayed with our daughter.

I thought I would never know the answer to these questions, but God always keeps His promises. In fact, I did not have long to wait at all.

Chapter 5:

The Letter

Early Tuesday morning, on March 8, 2005, Pastor Rick stopped by with a beautiful basket of flowers in one hand and a long envelope in the other.

Our pastor had a strange look on his face. Calmly, he asked me and Clark to sit down.

"You're gonna be amazed," he said.

We went into the living room and braced ourselves for the news. Pastor Rick started to share the events from earlier that morning.

He told us that someone from the Winter Garden Florist had contacted the church to confirm the upcoming funeral for "a Bethany Rivas."

After the receptionist said "yes," the florist then requested that the pastor come to the shop as soon as possible.

Apparently, the woman who had given our daughter CPR at the accident site had purchased flowers for the family.

More importantly, the Rev. Donna Weinheimer—as we soon learned her name—had also left a letter, which she wanted hand-delivered to Bethany's parents.

The following page contains an excerpt from the note.

Dear Rivas family and Justin:

You don't know me but I was with your daughter and friend Bethany at the end of her life as we know it.

I wanted to let you know that Bethany did not pass alone. I was with her, holding her and praying for her till she took her last breath.... She did not suffer and passed away peacefully.

It was not by chance that I was sitting outside at 11:00 that night and heard the crash, and it was not by chance that I responded to her needs....

Receiving this letter and knowing that God had answered my prayer helped me through the excruciating days after the accident.

Radiant Robes

Many people put in long hours preparing for Bethany's funeral, but one of the hardest parts for me was picking out her clothes to wear in the casket.

On Wednesday, Kristin and I drove to Justin's house which was about 10 minutes away. His parents, Donna and Randy, greeted us.

We hugged and shed some tears, then we began sharing memories. Some of them made us laugh; others made us cry.

Randy recalled once when Bethany was stranded and called him to fix her flat tire.

When I apologized for any inconvenience, he immediately replied that it was no problem at all. He had thought of her as a daughter.

Donna then shared how Bethany was always eager to help her unload the groceries, mainly so she could see what kind of cheese was in the bags. Kristin and I laughed since we knew cheese was her favorite food.

Finally, Donna, Kristin and I went into the bedroom to go through Bethany's clothes and choose what to take to the funeral home.

We decided she would be laid to rest in her favorite outfit: a pair of black pants with a blue, sparkly shirt.

Still laying on Bethany's pillow was a note Justin had given her before they went to the fair. In it he pledged his love and said he wanted her to be his wife.

I realized, with overwhelming grief, that if the accident had not happened, I would have been helping to pick out a gown for Bethany's wedding instead of clothes for her funeral.

Later that day, I did her laundry. I smelled her clothes before putting them in the washer, savoring her scent.

When I found a strand of her hair on a blouse, I held it and cried. It was all I had left of my beautiful daughter.

Along with dirty clothes, we had also brought home some with price tags still on them.

As I was folding her clean laundry, I was lamenting the fact that Bethany would *never* have the chance to wear her new ones.

Unaware God was listening to my thoughts, I was shocked when a voice suddenly interrupted me and said, "Bethany is clothed in *radiant robes of righteousness*! She does not need those filthy rags!"

I was filled with conflicting emotions. My fears about whether or not Bethany had returned to God were allayed. Yet, I deeply resented the fact that God had called her clean and brand new clothes "filthy rags."

We hadn't even buried her yet. I was reeling from pain and grief. My daughter and all of her belongings were precious to me. Why would God use such harsh words?

As I pondered the statement, a Bible verse came back to me that says, *All our righteousness are as **filthy rags** to God* (Isaiah 64:6).

Suddenly, I understood. Our earthly possessions mean nothing to God or to anyone who has crossed over.

Heaven's beauty far surpasses anything we could ever imagine. Our fancy, new outfits are as "filthy rags" to those who are clothed in radiant robes of righteousness!

Chapter 6:

Good Night Bethany

A few days before the funeral, family began arriving. First, was Clark's brother, John Rivas and his wife, Cecillia, along with their four children who came from Nashville.

Next, his parents, Richard and Evelyn Rivas, traveled from Albuquerque; his Uncle Lyman flew from Houston; and his Uncle John Calhoun came from California.

Since I am an only child, my closest family members were my uncle and aunt, David and Phyllis Folsom, who came from Colorado. My cousin, Karen Georgiades and her husband, Dan, flew in from Washington State.

Pam Gispert, a high school classmate who has been like a sister to me, drove from St. Petersburg with her husband, Rene, and their two children to support us.

The funeral was held on Friday, March 11, 2005, in our church's gymnasium.

An hour before the service, our family gathered in private at Bethany's coffin. We laid some mementos in it, including family pictures and the note from Justin asking her to marry him.

Kristin placed half of a Mizpah coin necklace in her sister's hand.

Mizpah necklaces come as a set for two people to share while they are separated. The halves of the coin read, "The Lord watch between me and thee while we are apart one from another." (Genesis 31:49)

We all lingered—hugging and crying—because we knew it would be the last time we would see her face.

After our time alone with Bethany, the funeral directors closed the coffin. Bethany's injuries had been very traumatic, so one of the most difficult decisions our family made was to have a closed casket.

On top of it, I placed an 8x10 photo of Bethany and Justin hugging, along with a framed letter from me. In it I wrote that I could not wait to see her again and that I was not saying *good-bye*...only *good night*.

Our family stood beside the casket as people filed by to pay their respects. We were amazed to see all 300 seats full and other guests standing in the back of the gym.

There were many young people in the congregation, including students from West Orange High School (located across the street from our church), as well as friends from the party my daughter had attended Sunday night.

I prayed their eyes would be opened to the dangers of drunk driving and to the fact that they can die at any time.

Just before the service began, an ambulance arrived with Justin and his parents. Covered with bruises and bandages, he sat in a wheelchair just a few feet from the coffin, which had the picture of him smiling with his arm around Bethany.

The service opened with my sister-in-law, Cecillia, singing "Grace Like Rain," [2] a contemporary version of the old hymn, "Amazing Grace."

I chose this song for Bethany because I knew God's grace had saved her. Although she had fallen away, she had given her heart to the Lord at a youth camp in 2003.

Some people believe once we are saved, even if we are not living for God, we can never lose our salvation.

Others believe it is possible to "backslide." Even though God always loves us, we can choose to stop loving Him and forsake His gift of salvation.

Either way, God fulfilled my request and sent someone to resuscitate my daughter and pray with her, until she could make peace with Him...and I would know it.

Next on the program was Bethany's former youth pastor, Charlie Dawes. He spoke about her vibrant personality, radiant smile and contagious laughter.

He even got a few chuckles when he mentioned her love of cheese—no matter what kind.

Kristin then approached the podium to share a few words about her sister.

She first told the story about getting stuck in a sewer grate when she was 3 and how Bethany said an alligator would probably eat her before their daddy could rescue her.

Then she spoke of the pain of hearing the news and the grief of having her older sister taken so soon.

Now, they would never take part in each other's weddings or see each other have babies.

There were tears in people's eyes as she told Bethany how much she missed her and how she hoped when she walked down the aisle someday, she would still be there in spirit.

Kristin promised to name her daughter after Bethany, if she had one, and then closed by saying, "Nothing will ever be the same without you here.

"May God grant us all grace, and to you, peace to rest in His arms, which have eternally longed for your return."

Before Pastor Rick preached, he read a letter Bethany had written to her sponsor who helped to pay her way to a Christian summer camp, called The Wilds, in 2003.

While attending camp, she rededicated her heart to the Lord and discovered she wanted to be in full-time ministry.

In the thank-you letter Bethany wrote to the sponsor, she said, "I feel a calling to travel and preach the Gospel."

It was for this reason that we asked Pastor Rick to preach a short message about the "prodigal son" who left home to try life on his own.

Luke 15:11-32 says that he spent months partying with his friends.

Eventually, when the city life had lost its excitement and his friends had vanished, he decided to return home but was afraid his father would disown him.

However, the Bible says when the father saw his son far off, he ran to meet him.

Pastor Rick explained that the parable illustrates how much God loves us.

No matter what we have done, He is longing for our return to Him. He is waiting for us, just as He was waiting for Bethany at that bend in the road.

In closing, our pastor asked anyone who was not sure where they would spend eternity to raise their hands and repeat the Prayer of Salvation with him. Many did.

I saw hands go up all over the church, and I realized Bethany's dream of winning souls for Christ was being fulfilled.

After the service, a long line of cars made their way to Woodlawn Cemetery in Gotha, a small town near Winter Garden, FL.

I had seen funeral processions before with patrol cars blocking intersections to let mourners journey unimpeded to that final resting place.

I had watched with a mixture of sadness, curiosity and impatience as I wondered who had died, how it had happened and how many more cars would go by.

I was always uncomfortable seeing the hearse and glad I was not riding in the "family car" behind it.

Now, it seemed inconceivable that the police officers were holding back traffic for *us*, and it was *my* daughter in the long, black car with curtains in the windows.

As I looked at the traffic backed up waiting for us to pass, I knew exactly what they were thinking.

The motorcade crept along, and we sat quietly for most of the way...until my husband broke the silence.

Since we had often teased Bethany for having a *lead foot*, Clark joked, "This is the first time I've been able to keep up with Bethany when she was in the car in front of me."

We all broke out in spontaneous laughter until he began to weep.

Clark shook his head and said brokenly, "I never thought I would be the one following behind a hearse with my daughter in it. I always thought I would die first and she would be following behind mine."

His words started everyone sobbing, especially Bethany's grandparents.

When we arrived at the graveside, I completely broke down. As I waited for her coffin to go into the ground, I just wanted to die and be with her.

I did not care that I had two other children. I did not want my daughter to be in the grave all alone.

Then the moment I dreaded finally came—the point where they would lower the coffin into the ground

Knowing that I would never see Bethany again, I wailed in anguish and buried my face against my Uncle David's shoulder. I would have collapsed if he had not held me up.

After a few minutes, I was finally able to compose myself. I leaned over and kissed her coffin. Then I softly whispered, "Good night, Bethany."

Momentary Lapse of Treason

Later that night, we heard the sounds of Kristin wailing. She said she could not bear to sleep in a warm, comfortable bed while Bethany was in the cold ground at the cemetery.

There was nothing Clark could do to comfort our younger daughter except lie beside her. Although Kristin was sobbing, I did not get out of bed. I am sure she has always wondered why.

The truth is, I could not. I was paralyzed with the worst pain and grief I have ever experienced.

Desperate, I screamed at God, *"WHY DIDN'T YOU RESCUE BETHANY? WHY DIDN'T YOU SAVE HER?"*

He answered gently, "I did." He gave no explanation and did not talk to me the rest of the night. It would be months before I understood His answer.

Meanwhile, I laid in bed, fighting guilt for being a bad mother...until I remembered that even Christ had lost one of His disciples.

Judas had lived with Jesus for three years, day and night, and he had heard and seen everything the other 11 did. However, because we all have free will, he chose to betray Christ—the Son of God, a perfect man and a perfect teacher.

His greed tempted him to hand over Jesus to the Pharisees for 30 pieces of silver, which he quickly regretted.

The Bible says he threw the money at their feet, went out and hung himself.

In a court of law, there is a phrase that describes someone who spontaneously does something which does not make rational sense. It is called a "temporary lapse of reason."

In his case, it was a *momentary lapse of treason*.

Bethany grew up in church and loved God all her life. She witnessed to friends—and even teachers—and invited many of them to church.

I will never forget what she told me the morning she moved out.

"Mom, I've been raised in the church all my life. I just want to try it awhile *without* God."

Believers sometimes stray away from Christ. But if and when this happens, He still provides a way back.

Knowing that God gave Bethany the opportunity to return to Him—like the father did the prodigal son in the Bible—gave me strength when the autopsy report came back the next month.

However, the night of the funeral, I was racked with despair. I spent the next few hours reliving the tumultuous events that caused Bethany to leave home a year and a half before her "untimely" death.

Chapter 7:

The Last Good-Bye

On Saturday morning, September 5, 2005, five days after Bethany's 18th birthday, she moved out of our home and in with her boyfriend, Justin, and his family.

This "move" did not take us completely by surprise. The night before had been turbulent.

On Friday evening, she had blatantly disobeyed her father, so he grounded her for a month. Angry, she cussed us out and reminded us that she was now 18 and no longer had to "obey" our rules.

Her father then reminded her that she still lived under our roof...so as long as we supported her...she would have to abide by our rules.

Bethany stormed out of the house around 11 p.m. and about an hour later, Clark called the police. Since she was 18, there was nothing they could do.

Shortly afterward, our neighbors, Dave and Trish, called to tell us that Bethany was at their house. She eventually came home, apologized and went to bed.

The next morning, our family went out for breakfast, as we often did on Saturdays. Bethany, however, claimed she was "exhausted" and wanted to sleep in.

After breakfast, we decided to take in a movie and hoped Bethany would accompany us.

When we pulled into the driveway, our "exhausted" daughter was vigorously helping Justin's brother load his pickup truck with all her worldly possessions.

We were stunned but stayed and helped load the rest of her things. Although we were adamant against her decision, we realized we could do nothing about it.

For the first three months, we did not communicate with her. Kristin saw her at school and they remained close, but Bethany was not allowed in our home. Her father even changed the locks.

Finally, Clark and I agreed to visit a Christian counselor for advice on how to reconcile with our daughter.

My husband had a long list of things Bethany had to change before he forgave her and allowed her back home.

The counselor listened politely and then asked, "What changes did God require before He agreed to forgive us and let us into His kingdom?"

Clark and I sat silently, realizing God had accepted and loved us unconditionally.

My husband tore up his list, and we went to see Bethany. He asked her to forgive him and told her that she was always welcome at home.

Bethany then pulled a letter out of her purse that she had written weeks before, asking for our forgiveness. She said she had been afraid to give it to us.

After Clark and I read the letter, we all hugged and cried.

Although Bethany did not move back home, she and Justin became a part of our family again.

We spent many happy times together, especially on holidays and vacations.

10/21/03

Dear Mom & Dad,
    I can't begin to tell you how sorry I am for all the trouble & hurt I've caused you. I never wanted to leave on such bad terms. Please don't think that I hate you because I truly love you both very much. I am very thankful for my years under your guidance and love. I am extremly lucky to have had such caring parents in my life. I am sorry for everything I did and said. I am responsible for my actions so please don't think that y'all did Nothing wrong. I do miss you and the family. I hope someday y'all can 4give me. I am working at the new Eckerds on 535 by Winn Dixie. The official grand opening is on Clints b-day, Oct. 5th. There will be many sales if you'd like to stop by. I hope we can see eachother soon. Once again I apologize for everything.

                    I love you,
                    Bethany
                    Rivas

45

One day, Clark stopped by Bethany's new job at Starbucks to invite her and Justin to a play that Kristin's boyfriend would be in that weekend.

She accepted the invitation and made her dad an extra large cup of coffee with about 4 inches of whipped cream on top. It was so tall, he could barely carry it, much less drink it.

But that was Bethany, fun loving and generous.

Bethany poses with her dad at the Church of the Nazarene General Assembly June 2002 in Indianapolis.

On Friday night, Bethany and Justin met Clark and Kristin at a nearby church to watch the play. Since Clint and I had seen it the weekend before, we stayed home and watched a movie about Ray Charles. Even this was prophetic.

In the story, Ray's little brother drowns and his mother throws herself on the coffin and wails during the funeral. The scene was so gut-wrenching, I cried.

My son, who was 12 years old at the time, looked at me sympathetically. I could tell he was puzzled as to why the movie had affected me so profoundly.

I remember telling him, "Clint, until you have children of your own, you will never fully understand a parent's love and how devastating it would be to bury a part of yourself."

Little did I know that I would face the excruciating reality of this experience 48 hours later.

At the play, Bethany ran into many of her old friends from the youth group she was part of at church.

After she had stopped going, she complained that none of the members had called or come by and felt they had turned their backs on her. Yet, she never contacted them either.

Eighteen months had passed with Bethany thinking her friends wanted nothing to do with her, while they were also thinking the same thing.

That evening, the pastor and his wife, and most of the youth group, attended the play. They had a chance to see Bethany and catch up on old times.

During intermission, there was a vendor who was selling books, so Clark asked Bethany to pick one as a gift for Mother's Day.

My husband said she perused through several before choosing a devotional titled *Boundless Love*, which is full of true stories about God's unconditional love.

He purchased the book and tucked it away, then gave it to me on Mother's Day *after* Bethany died.

Around 10 p.m., after the play was finished, Clark called to say everyone was hungry and coming to our house to eat. I jumped off the sofa and began heating up some leftovers.

My husband, along with our daughters and their boyfriends, arrived about 20 minutes later.

I had missed Bethany a lot, and it was always a privilege to see her. We still kept in touch regularly and had spent many wonderful times together, even after she left home.

That night, she asked me if I had hung up any of the new family pictures on the wall. These photos were another blessing from God.

I've heard that people sometimes have a premonition of their death. I wonder if my daughter had one because of something she said the day we took the family portrait.

Our church had scheduled photo sessions for the new directory, and even though Bethany had never attended Faith Family Community Church, she agreed to join us.

As luck—or rather providence—would have it, we were the last family of the day, so the photographer offered to take additional poses to use up his film.

He snapped pictures of me and Clark; the three children; Bethany and Kristin; and then several of Bethany and Justin.

When we viewed the proofs, the saleswoman tried to persuade us to purchase the complete package. However, with Christmas just over, our funds were depleted.

I requested only the free 8x10, but Bethany insisted on ordering the package.

"Mom, this may be the *last* time we get to take a family photo." Her statement made no sense at the time.

"Of course we will have other opportunities," I said. "We'll have *the rest of our lives* to take another portrait but, right now, I'm broke!"

Bethany was determined. She pulled out her checkbook and offered to pay half.

I knew she didn't have a lot of money, so when I saw how serious she was, I agreed to buy the package and make payments.

The photos had just arrived in the mail and were sitting on the coffee table unopened.

After everyone ate, I cleared off the kitchen table while Bethany and Kristin went in the living room to look at the new pictures.

Immediately, a heavy feeling came over me to quit cleaning and go into the living room with them. Yet, this went against everything I had been taught as a child.

I had been raised to finish my work first and then relax, so I pushed on, ignoring the feeling in my gut.

Suddenly, I remembered the birthday card Bethany had given me a month prior that said, "Although you seldom say I love you...."

Realizing how I had often put "getting things done" ahead of spending time with my children, I thought, *Bethany is hardly ever here anymore. I should spend these last few minutes today with her.*

Believe it or not, instead of stopping, I rushed to put the rest of the plates in the dishwasher.

I was almost finished when a literal voice in my head shouted, "STOP DOING THE DISHES AND SPEND TIME WITH YOUR DAUGHTER!!!!"

A bolt of electricity shot through me. The voice was so loud and demanding that it startled me. Right away I knew it was God.

The voice had said, "YOUR DAUGHTER." I would not say that to myself.

I did not know why it was so imperative that I be with her. Perhaps Bethany needed to know I loved her more than cleaning the kitchen.

There was a slight knot in my stomach. I had been getting a lot of strange feelings about her lately and they had me worried.

I dropped the rag in the sink, without even rinsing or wringing it out, and hurried into the living room.

For 30 minutes, my daughters and I cut out 4x7 photos and put them in frames on the fireplace mantel.

As Bethany was about to leave, *something* in my spirit said, "Tell her you love her."

Although I seldom say those words when there was no particular reason, I didn't argue. I walked over, put my arms around her and whispered, "I love you, Bethany!"

She was taken by surprise but then a huge grin spread across her face as she threw her arms around me.

"I love you too, Mom!" she said beaming.

We gave each other a big, tight, bear hug. Then she and Justin walked to the door.

Before opening it, she paused and asked if I still wanted to meet her Tuesday night at the Borders bookstore—like we did so often to share a Mocha Frappuccino and read together.

Justin had been on school break for a couple weeks, so she and I had also taken a break. I assured her that I definitely wanted to start up again.

When she reached the driveway, I shouted, "See ya at Borders!"

Bethany turned around, waved cheerfully and then called out, "See ya Tuesday!"

Her words would haunt me 17 days later...on Tuesday.

See Ya Tuesday

Oftentimes, when you hear of spirits contacting the living, they are usually relegated to stories of haunted houses, and normally they frighten you—not comfort you. This story is different.

The night I believe Bethany "visited" our home, I was not frightened. I was amazed, yes, but I knew instinctively she had come back to comfort me and say good-bye.

My last image of her alive will always be her smiling face as she turned around and waved cheerfully, "See ya Tuesday!"

Two weeks after Bethany died, I had returned to work and immediately threw myself into processing the contracts that had piled up. I tried not to think about my loss. But the shock and denial continued for some time.

As I drove home the third Tuesday after Bethany died, I absent-mindedly pulled into the Borders parking lot (like I had done so many times before) and walked into the store.

It only took one look at the coffee shop and the empty table where Bethany usually sat to remind me that she was gone—and she would *never* meet me there again.

I burst into tears and practically ran to my car. I got in, sobbing uncontrollably, unable to drive home. I called my husband, who had taken our son to karate practice, and begged him to pick me up.

Clark was at least 30 minutes away and since Clint's lesson had already started, he urged me to try and make it home.

I sat in the parking lot another 15 minutes. Then I slowly drove home, constantly wiping my eyes.

The house was dark and quiet, except for the welcoming bark of our dog, Rex, who loved to greet us at the front door.

When I reached down to pat him, he stopped barking and laid his ears back, as he always did, so I could rub the top of his head.

Rex followed me to the office and curled up beside me as I turned on the computer.

Perhaps it was that moment at Borders when the reality of Bethany's death finally penetrated the shroud of shock and denial that was wrapped so tightly around me.

I sat at the computer, and still sobbing, pounded away at the keys as I wrote her a letter. My words were angry and filled with desperation and grief.

"HOW COULD YOU DO THIS TO US???? WHY DID YOU LEAVE ME LIKE THIS???? WHY DID YOU GO TO THAT STUPID PARTY??? WHY DID YOU GET INTO THAT CAR???? WHERE ARE YOU NOW, BETHANY????"

I typed for about 10 minutes, pouring out my thoughts. Rex was sleeping quietly.

Suddenly, he jumped up and started barking, as if someone was at the door.

I figured it was Clark and since he had a key, I kept typing. Rex, however, continued to bark.

I wondered why Clark hadn't come in. Then I noticed that our dog had not gone to the front door.

Instead, he was barking and staring directly at the family portrait we had just taken. He continued to look at it, specifically at Bethany, and bark.

I walked to the front door. No one was there.

Unsettled, I returned to the office, grabbed Rex by the collar and pulled him over to my chair.

Usually a calm and obedient dog, it surprised me when he instantly wrenched himself free and returned to sit across the room, barking again at the picture.

I turned on the light to see if there was a fly on the wall but there were no bugs anywhere.

Suddenly, he stopped barking and laid his ears back and put his head down like he does when we pet him.

He kept his ears down and head lowered for several minutes. It was as if an *unseen hand* was gently stroking him.

I sat in the chair and watched in amazement. Rex finally raised his head and continued staring at the picture. It was then that I noticed the soft *glow* around Bethany.

I'm sure the lighter area on the background canvas was to help the photographer center people but it made Bethany look like she had, indeed, gone on to become an "angel."

The last family portrait taken for our church directory two months before Bethany died.

There was no mistake that Rex was staring at the picture. It was quite high on the wall and his eyes remained glued to the center of it—at Bethany's face. Although it was definitely eerie, I was not afraid.

"Rex, do you see Bethany?" I repeated this question several times. He slowly raised his eyes till they rested on a point on the ceiling.

Again, he remained stiff and focused, staring intently at a blank spot.

I looked with him but couldn't see anything or anyone. Whatever he was staring at must have disappeared because he returned to my side, curled up and went back to sleep.

The next day, I told Crystal's mother, Candy, about the incident.

She said hearing about Rex gave her chills because a similar thing had happened with Crystal's dog a few days after the funeral.

Then she asked, "Sharon, didn't you tell me the last thing Bethany said was that she would see you on Tuesday?"

"Yes," I replied.

"Yesterday was Tuesday," Candy exclaimed. "I think Bethany wanted you to know she kept her promise."

I believe she did.

Chapter 8:

The Fire and the Furnace

In the days after Bethany's death, God used two messages to speak to me. Although it had been years since I heard them, He brought them back clearly to my memory.

The first one was taught by my mother during children's church when I was 10 years old.

Holding a large picture book called *Little Red Hen*, she told us about a mother hen who smelled smoke and sensed impending danger.

The hen clucked out a warning to her baby chicks and gathered them under her wings.

One little chick refused to come, however. He saw no danger. He was curious about the bright, red lights dancing in the distance.

No matter how urgently his mother clucked for him to come to her, he refused to listen. Instead, he headed toward the flames.

The next day, as the farmer went through the ashes, he found the scorched mother hen, still sitting on her nest. He was puzzled.

He was sure she could have sought safety and wondered why she had stayed. Then he heard chirping and realized that, hidden safely under her wings, was her flock of chicks.

After looking closer, the farmer noticed one was missing. He searched through the debris and found the missing chick far away from his mother.

The chick had died needlessly in the fire, simply because he did not take heed to her warning.

My mother said this was an illustration of Matthew 23:37 where Jesus looked out on the city of Jerusalem and wept,

O Jerusalem, Jerusalem...how often I have wanted to gather your children together as a hen protects her chicks beneath her wings, but you would not let me.

She reminded us that Christ sacrificed His life on the cross so that everyone could come to Him and be saved but, sadly, not everyone does.

The pictures of the loving mother hen who had sacrificed her life to save her chicks and the rebellious baby chick affected me deeply.

As a young girl sitting in children's church, I wondered if I would be willing to give my life to save any of my children when I grew up.

Now as a mother, the fact that I had not saved Bethany haunted me.

Even though I had offered my life to God in exchange for hers the night she died, He would not negate her free will.

Suddenly I understood why Jesus wept in Matthew 23:37.

Thankfully, a message I heard when Bethany was a toddler returned to comfort me. It was preached by Pastor Keith Wright at Kansas City First Church of the Nazarene.

Titled "The Fourth Man," the sermon was about the three Hebrew boys who were thrown into a fiery furnace because they refused to bow down and worship the king.

The heat of the furnace was so hot that the guards who threw them in perished.

However, the king noticed that the three Israelites were walking around in the fire and with them was a *fourth* man who appeared to be the Son of God.

Pastor Wright stressed that, although there would come a time when we would be placed in the furnace, we would not be alone. God would be with us!

He closed with Isaiah 43:2, *When you walk through the fire, you will not be burned*.

I was so moved by the message that I bought the tape and listened to it repeatedly in the kitchen while I washed dishes. Bethany was a year old, and I was pregnant with Kristin.

I can still see Bethany with her thick glasses, scooting around the kitchen on a little yellow bus.

The wheels squeaked so loudly that I was constantly turning up the volume on the tape player in order to hear the sermon.

Eighteen years later, I was amazed to hear my pastor, Rev. Rick Page, preach the *same* message titled "The Fourth Man" in February 2005.

Once more, it was as if a lightning bolt hit me. I felt impressed to listen *carefully*.

The message was being given to me…again…for a reason. Once more the words, "When you walk through the fire" captured my attention.

My spirit quickened as my pastor talked about *the Fourth Man—Christ—*who will stand with us in the furnace.

"We may face trials and tragedies," Pastor Rick told the congregation, "but God would face them with us and give us strength."

As I had done when Bethany was a child, I ordered a copy of the message. Yet, I hoped I would never have to *walk through the fire* or be placed in a furnace.

The next Sunday, my daughter was killed.

Premonitions

As days went by, we heard more and more stories from other family members about their premonitions on that fatal night in March 2005.

Clark's dad was sitting in church when he had an overwhelming feeling that something bad was going to happen to one of his family members.

Unable to concentrate on the sermon, he left the service and went to his car to be alone. He was not sure who needed prayer, but he knew God was telling him to pray.

The next morning, he discovered it was Bethany.

God also spoke to my Aunt Eileen who lived in Kentucky. She was getting ready for church that night when, suddenly, she felt the urgency to pray.

My cousin, Wes, arrived to pick her up, but she told him she could not leave. God was telling her to pray for the soul of a loved one who needed to be saved.

She seemed so concerned that Wes stayed and prayed with her for an hour instead of going to the worship service.

The next morning, Aunt Eileen received the news and realized they had been praying for Bethany.

It is clear that God knew our daughter was going to die.

Since we all have free will, the Lord always gives us opportunities to make choices...but He already knows what decisions we will make.

Before Bethany left the party to go to the store, she was told by several others not to get in the car because the driver had been drinking.

A friend of Crystal, the other victim, opened the car door and told them to get out. He said he had a bad feeling about them riding with Steven.

Even Justin's mom said she had a bad feeling that night. She actually called Justin and told him to make sure he and Bethany left the birthday party by 9 p.m., because she feared something would happen if they stayed longer.

We later learned it was around 10 p.m. when they headed to the store on a winding, country road. If they had obeyed his mom, Bethany would still be alive and Justin would not have been injured.

God sent several people to warn my daughter and give her opportunities to choose correctly.

However, since He had told me a month before to save the knickknacks she had given me *in case something happened to her*, He knew she would not listen.

I believe the Lord always knows ahead of time how we will choose, which is why He told me to stop cleaning and spend time with her on that last Friday we had together.

God also gave me a choice in what to do with the knick-knacks.

He did not tell me she would die (*of course, then I would have kept the vases*). Instead, He only said "if." That way, it was still my decision.

I made the right choice when I saved them but made the wrong choice to erase her beautiful voicemail messages, which I now deeply regret.

Another significant event that shows God's hand moving in this situation involved Clark's brother and sister-in-law who lived in Nashville.

John and Cecillia owned a timeshare near Sea World in Orlando. Whenever they did not use it, Cecillia would post it on the Internet and their week would sell immediately.

Several months before Bethany died, they decided to remodel their home. To raise money for this project, they agreed to rent the timeshare the week of March 6, 2005.

However, when John and Cecillia advertised their timeshare, they did not get a single bite. They even lowered the price, thinking that would work.

Cecillia later admitted that she was upset with God for not helping them out.

It wasn't until Clark called and told them Bethany had been killed that my in-laws realized the significance of having that week.

Their family of six was able to attend the funeral and stay in their timeshare because it had *not* been rented.

They thought they weren't going to use it that year. Obviously, God knew otherwise, which is why He *helped them keep it.*

Trapped

A few days after the funeral, my Aunt Margaret called and said God told her Bethany was trapped in something she felt she couldn't get out of. I had no idea what that meant.

I also had not understood when God told me, the night of the funeral, that He had *rescued* Bethany.

Although He did not explain at the time, I realize now, it would have been too painful to hear.

A week later, Clint and I were at home watching TV. As I flipped through the channels, we came across the Oprah Winfrey Show.

Instead of Oprah sitting on a stage interviewing guests, her camera crew was following the activities of a high school girl who was addicted to methamphetamines.

The camera crew was staying at her home and taping her erratic behavior.

The girl went for days without sleep and suffered such severe withdrawals and cravings that she was "climbing the walls."

She constantly begged her parents to let her out of the house so she could get another fix.

When they refused, she threatened to kill herself because she couldn't take the torture anymore.

It was so horrifying that I actually turned to Clint and said, "I would rather have buried Bethany than to have her ever addicted to meth."

A month later, the autopsy showed alcohol, speed, *meth* and marijuana in Bethany's blood.

There was no question about it. The birthday party she had attended had also been a drug party.

After learning about the autopsy, I was *sick*...then *livid*. How could Bethany do something so dangerous and stupid? Why would she even try something so addictive?

Although someone told us it was the first time she had tried it, we later learned she may have attended similar parties.

The Internet is full of websites warning that crystal meth is more addictive than crack cocaine or heroine! Research also shows that trying to overcome a meth addiction is almost impossible.

Some months later, my friend, John, who knew about the autopsy report, forwarded an email to me.

It was so heartbreaking that I feel compelled to share a short excerpt from it.

My Name Is Meth

I destroy homes. I tear families apart,
Take your children, and that's just the start.
I'm more costly than diamonds, more precious than gold,
The sorrow I bring is a sight to behold.

I have many names, but there's one you know best.
I'm sure you've heard of me, my name is Meth.
My power is awesome; try me you'll see,
But if you do, you may never break free.

Just try me once and I might let you go,
But try me twice, and I'll own your soul.
When I possess you, you'll steal and lie.
You'll do what you have to just to get high.

I take kids from parents, and parents from kids,
I turn people from God and separate friends.
I'll take everything from you, your looks and your pride,
I'll be with you always—right by your side.

I'll be your master, you'll be my slave.
I'll even go with you, when you go to your grave.
Now that you have met me, what will you do?
Will you try me or not? It's all up to you.

I can bring you more misery than words can tell,
Come take my hand, let me lead you to hell.

It took weeks before I could face the possibility that Bethany may have been leading a double life.

She was interviewing for a supervisory position at Starbucks, and we were told at the funeral that she was favored to get it.

To us, her future was looking up, but she may have been secretly choosing a path that was leading her down a one-way street…to a dead end.

It doesn't matter how well your child does in school, how great they are doing at work or how happy they seem. Methamphetamine abuse is becoming a drug problem of epidemic proportions among "nice" kids.

It's cheap, easy to get and easy to make, and it's going to destroy our children if we don't wake up!

You cannot *tell* if they've tried it. My family couldn't. The Fischers couldn't.

Even good kids get tempted by their peers to try the drug "just once," but that is all it takes to become hopelessly…helplessly…addicted.

Bethany's future, if she had lived and continued on the same course, is not one I dare to contemplate. It's too unbearable.

Although our family did not know what was going on, God did, and He sees death differently than we do. He knows it frees us from sickness, suffering, addiction or anything else that has us *trapped*.

Now, I finally understood why God said He rescued her, but I was still in turmoil. We had raised Bethany in a loving Christian home.

What went wrong?

Chapter 9:

Looking Back

Parents who lose a child tend to look back and wonder what could have been done differently to save their son or daughter. My husband and I are no exception.

One day, we were eating dinner when Clark told our son he realized, now, that a lot of the issues he thought were so important with Bethany really weren't.

She wanted a tattoo and we said "no!" Clark had been adamant about not letting her get another ear piercing, which was the main reason she moved out. Of course, she didn't want to go to church or have a curfew either.

As parents, we have to choose our battles and do the very best we can to raise our children.

Religious beliefs and safety issues are important, but the number of earrings or tattoos isn't worth losing a son or daughter over.

In the end, I think behavior may have more to do with the child's own temperament.

Siblings growing up in the same home often turn out differently. Their likes and dislikes are different. Their personalities and behaviors are different.

Sometimes, this leads to worrying more about one child and applying stricter rules to one over the other.

I believe Bethany may have felt that we were easier on Kristin and even favored her more.

The truth is, however, we tried harder to protect our oldest child because she was the one who usually got into trouble.

One summer, when Bethany was 5 and Kristin was 3, we attended a district assembly and stayed at a hotel in Houston.

Clark and I went to the pool and put flotation rings on our girls. We told them firmly to stay in the shallow end.

They were sitting on the steps playing happily in the water, while we sat in the chairs, just a few feet away.

All of a sudden, Clark glanced over to see Bethany's flotation ring gone. Her eyes searched for help as she began to sink slowly below the water near the deep end.

He shouted, "*BETHANY'S DROWNING!*"

Immediately I dove in and pulled her out. Everyone at the pool rushed over and after several seconds of coughing and sputtering, she regained consciousness.

When we asked Kristin, who was still sitting obediently on the steps, why she hadn't told us that her sister was paddling toward the deep end, she said, "Bethany made me promise not to tell."

Incidences like this repeated themselves many times over the years—different scenarios but the same principle.

Several years before Bethany met Justin, we had to take the computer out of her room because Clark caught her looking at homosexual porn.

Kristin knew about it, but her older sister had made her promise not to tell. Clint, who was seven years younger than Bethany, was not so easily persuaded.

One time, she snuck a girl—who she wasn't allowed to see—into her room and they smoked something that smelled *funny*, according to Clint.

He told his dad, despite Bethany's plea not to say anything. Of course, she was grounded.

However, it seems like she was trying to live up to the name embroidered on the leopard fur pillow she had bought for her bed that read, "WILD CHILD."

Bethany's room shows her love for leopards & tigers.

Wild Child

Like any teenager, Bethany thought we were suffocating her with our rules. We only had a few but we enforced them.

We told her and Kristin not to take drugs and not to hang around others who did. They also had a curfew and had to call us if they were going to be late.

Before our daughters were 18, they were not allowed to be with a boy alone unless they were at his home and a parent was there, or they had to double date. And, of course, they were required to attend church with us.

These "rules," I believe, are normal for most Christian homes. And because we are Christians, our belief system did not allow for any homosexual behavior.

This is the one area I wonder if we should have handled differently.

Our family never tolerated prejudice of any kind. Clark and I worked with people of different races, religions and sexual orientation. Many of them were good friends, and Bethany knew we were receptive and loving to everyone.

However, after Clark caught her reading an explicit lesbian novel and she admitted to having a romantic relationship with a "girlfriend" at school, we were very upset and immediately told her to end it.

Bethany became angry and confused about her feelings toward God as well as herself. She thought she could not be a Christian and have homosexual feelings.

Perhaps this thinking caused her to turn to an alternative lifestyle, other than the one she had been raised in.

Nevertheless, Bethany's relationship with girls may have been a fad because later she fell in love with Justin. But her rebellious behavior escalated when we cut her off from her gay friends.

I have asked myself repeatedly, "Should we have been more accepting?"

This experience has definitely taught me how difficult it is for families that have to confront homosexuality. I am much more understanding and sympathetic now.

In the weeks following Bethany's death, I thought a lot about her upbringing and early years.

It seemed only yesterday she had been a beautiful, bubbly little girl. Even as a child, she had been very spiritual.

I tried to think back. *When had things changed?*

Grandma Battin spends time with Bethany.

Rivas Family photo taken
in Houston, Texas 1991.

Bethany poses with her younger siblings,
Kristin and Clint.

Chapter 10:

Bethany

Bethany was always an energetic ray of sunshine. Her contagious laughter had been an identifying characteristic ever since she was little.

I remember when she was 15 months old. We were living in Kansas City, Missouri.

Clark was attending seminary, and my mother had flown in from Florida to help me.

Kristin was just born, and I was rocking her in the living room while my mother was washing dishes in the adjoining kitchen.

Grandma Curtis lends a helping hand.

Bethany was toddling around, playing with toys when she broke out into a series of delightful giggles, clapping her hands with glee.

Bethany giggles with Mom and baby sister.

My mother said, "Oh my, listen to that tinkling little laughter.

"I can just hear her when she grows up. She's going to be the life of every party." She was right—Bethany was!

Although my daughter loved to laugh and have fun, she could also be very sensitive and tenderhearted.

One day, I was giving her a bath when I began crying over something that was troubling me.

Bethany, who was about 1 year old, stared at me intently. Then she looked as if she was going to cry.

She could barely talk but she leaned over, put her arms around me and said in the sweetest voice, "Love Mommy. Love Mommy."

She took her little hands and pulled up the corners of my mouth to make me smile.

I grinned, but then I broke down and wept even harder as I gathered her into my arms. Her small act of love had touched me so deeply that this time, I wept with joy.

Bethany was always an animal lover. Over the years, she had a string of fish; mice; gerbils; turtles; hermit crabs; kittens; and dogs.

Occasionally, she had a few of them, all at the same time, but settled on cats (of all kinds) as her favorite pet.

As a teenager, she wallpapered her room in tiger stripes, complete with leopard spot decor and pictures of lions.

She was also curious about everything, as demonstrated by an incident with her hermit crabs.

Bethany had just gotten two crabs for her 10th birthday, and she and Kristin were playing with them.

Suddenly, Kristin noticed that her sister's crab had disappeared.

When she asked Bethany where it was, she popped it out of her mouth and held it up to show Kristin that it was safe.

Kristin stormed into the kitchen and yelled, "Mom, Bethany just put a hermit crab in her mouth! She's probably gonna get sick and die!"

Horrified, I ran into the bedroom and asked her why on earth had she done such a thing.

As best as Kristin and I can recall, Bethany said she did it because she wanted to see how it felt to have the crab crawl around inside her mouth.

Kristin and Bethany

Although they were each other's best friend growing up, Bethany and Kristin were very different.

The "Tom Boy" and the "Princess" would best describe them.

Once, Kristin's kindergarten teacher asked me if our religion required girls to wear only dresses.

She was concerned because my daughter came to school every day in frilly dresses and lacy socks, and she didn't want to see them get ripped or dirty.

I assured her that I had tried repeatedly to coax Kristin to wear her cute little pants outfits, but she would have nothing to do with them.

Bethany was a different story, however. Getting her to wear a dress as a child, for even one hour on Sunday, was a struggle.

This was because she loved to climb trees in the churchyard and had a hard time doing it in a dress. We had forbidden her to do it, of course, but that never stopped her.

Invariably, Kristin would dutifully come and get us after church, and we would find Bethany up a tree as her first-grade Sunday school class cheered her on.

Consequently, she was the one who *usually* ripped her dresses and dirtied her socks.

Bethany was also very active. It may be hard to believe, but when she was 7, she asked us to buy her a set of exercise equipment.

We searched around and actually found some aerobic items for children.

Our family had a standing joke about the way she would don a workout leotard, pop in a Jane Fonda tape and lie on a mat, sweating with two little weights in hand.

Meanwhile, Kristin would relax on the couch, eating Twinkies, and give her older sister pointers.

"Bethany, you're not lifting your legs high enough. You should touch the floor when you bend over. You're cheating."

At some point, Bethany would catch the irony of it all and holler for me to make Kristin be quiet.

Another thing people remember about Bethany, besides her boisterous laughter, radiant smile and obsessive love of cheese, was the fact that she was extremely generous.

When she was 14 years old, she read about a little girl who had leukemia and needed an additional $2,000 to finish paying for a bone marrow transplant.

Bethany asked one of her 8th grade teachers, Mr. Peters, if the class could try to raise the funds.

He told her that the students would *never* come up with this kind of money, and even if they could, they would not make the two-week deadline.

Bethany was so determined that she vowed to do it herself. Her teacher was so sure she couldn't pull it off that he promised to let her shave his head if she succeeded.

She worked hard and recruited our entire family to help her. She baked cookies, and I took them to work and sold them for $5 each or 3 for $10.

Because it was for a good cause, everyone complied with a smile and joked that they were the most expensive cookies they had ever bought.

Bethany also had her father get the company he worked for, as well as members of our church, to donate a large sum.

Toward the end of the first week, she bought water bottles on sale for 50 cents and sold them for $2 or $3 at a soccer game on Friday.

It was a blistering hot day, and the water was selling great. Bethany, however, refused to drink any, as she was saving every bottle to raise money for the little girl.

Halfway through the game, she passed out from heat exhaustion. An ambulance was called and people gathered around, asking why she had not drunk any of the water.

When they heard the story about her fund raising efforts, parents, teachers and other students got involved. At the end of the two weeks, she had the $2,000.

A photographer from the *Orlando Sentinel* newspaper was on hand to take a picture of Bethany shaving Mr. Peters' head.

Close shave

Lakeview Middle School student Bethany Rivas, 14, uses electric clippers to give teacher Paul Peters a buzz cut Wednesday. Peters winces as the clippers mow a path through his locks. The teacher had said if the students raised $2,000 for the Leukemia Society he would let them shave his head. They did.

Used with permission of the *Orlando Sentinel*. Copyright © 1999.

Bethany loved holidays and special occasions, and she always wanted to organize a big celebration.

At age 13, she asked me what her dad and I were doing for our anniversary. I told her things were a little tight, so we were just going to eat at the house.

When Clark and I arrived home from work, romantic music was playing, and candles and china were on the dining room table.

Since the kitchen was open to the adjoining dining room, Bethany had attached a piece of string to nails and strung a bed sheet across the doorway.

She had 6-year-old Clint in his Easter suit acting as maitre d', complete with a mustache that she had drawn on with mascara.

He had a little towel slung over his arm and was holding menus his sister had typed on the computer.

THE RIVAS PLACE TO EAT

*Special of the day: In between this egg omelet we find cheesy chunks of cheese. On the outside of this cheese we find juicy eggs. Toped off with a special sauce, this would be a delight any time of the day. Side(s) include: toast, purple grapes, and a variety of yogurt.

DINNER

The Turkey Meal- this delicious white meat comes with gravy and dressing, the softest mashed potatoes and fresh peas to please your every taste bud.

The Salisbury Steak Meal- this tasty piece of steak is drenched in delicate gravy, with fabulous mashed potatoes, and juicy, buttered corn made to perfection.

The Sliced Beef Meal- these slices of beef come from the finest cows in the country. Served with the softest mashed potatoes and freshest, green peas that will satisfy your hunger.

*Substitute your meat for scrumptious, golden fried chicken.

DESSERTS

Not only does our chef make marvelous meals but also the finest desserts are provided to quench that sweet tooth of yours.

Jell-O: A variety of flavors including lime, cherry, strawberry and raspberry seem to make your mouth bounce with joy. Topped with whipped cream and a choice of sugared marshmallows.

DRINKS

The special drink of the house tonight is the *Welch's Red Grape Juice. Served chilled and non-alcoholic, this makes a great compliment for any age with our spectacular desserts.

We have pure, clear *water* served from the freshest of springs.

Milk from the finest of cows in all the land is served cold right here. Also comes in chocolate.

Bethany had rummaged through the fridge and did her best to come up with several meals she hoped she could cook.

They were advertised on the menu, using the fanciest language she could think of such as "milk from the finest cows in all the land" and "topped with special sauce" (which turned out to be ketchup with pepper).

When we weren't exactly sure about one of the meals, we asked the waitress, Kristin, to explain a little bit more about the dish.

She rolled her eyes and said with exasperation, "I have no idea...and you guys don't even want to see the kitchen. There's stuff all over the walls!"

Even after Bethany moved in with Justin, she went out of her way to make celebrations special for us.

On my 46th birthday, a year before her death, she woke up at 5 a.m. to drive over and catch her dad before he left on his long-distance truck route. (This was a big deal because she preferred to sleep in.)

Bethany wanted to see if he had planned something for me that day. Since he hadn't had time to do anything yet, he gave her money to go shopping.

She surprised me at work with flowers and a birthday cake. Later that evening, she and her boyfriend came over to cook a delicious dinner for me.

Perhaps Bethany's greatest asset was her sense of humor. One summer, she accompanied us to a timeshare in Fort Lauderdale and pulled a stunt that we have laughed about ever since.

When we arrived that night and saw the buildings, we were hesitant to go inside, fearing it was just as old and run down as the outside.

Clark asked me to check it out and immediately Bethany offered to go with me. That was normal.

From the time she was a child, she always volunteered to go with me everywhere.

I think it was because Bethany was adventurous and loved to explore. Now, she was eager to accompany me once more.

When we opened the door to the timeshare, we discovered the inside had been newly remodeled.

It turned out to be a beautiful townhouse with a large balcony and backyard pool.

I was relieved to know everyone would be surprised. Bethany, however, did not want to waste the opportunity to pull a practical joke on the family.

"Let's fool them, Mom. Let's tell them the place is a dump so they'll be *really* shocked when they see it."

With some reservations, I accompanied her back to the parking lot and let her do the talking. She went on and on, regaling them with how terrible it looked inside.

Bethany even claimed that she noticed an area of dried blood on the carpet, insinuating it may have been the scene of foul play.

Horrified, Clark promptly told everyone to get back in the car so we could look for a hotel.

As hard as she tried, she could not convince her dad and the others to go inside and view "the blood."

Finally, I had to step in and assure them she was teasing.

When everyone saw how nice the place was, they were definitely shocked, and Bethany was delighted that her ruse had been such a success.

Bethany, Kristin and Clint

Before she left her faith as a teenager, Bethany had also been an avid evangelist. She invited many of her high school friends, including her boyfriend, to church with us.

Justin attended for many months, and he and Clint were baptized together. His mother and I sat beside each other, and I remember feeling so happy and proud.

The next week, however, Bethany turned 18 and left the church. Even after she left, there were five or six teenagers she had invited who continued to attend.

Needless to say, they were the ones who were most surprised by the sudden change in her behavior.

We learned later from notes she had written to friends that her desire to leave the church was a result of being curious about life and wanting her freedom, rather than her lack of faith.

Bethany, according to her good friend Brittany, often said that she could never deny the existence of God. She knew He was real. She had seen too many miracles.

Great Faith

As a child, Bethany's faith was so strong that it amazed me and actually put me to shame.

She knew she had been severely cross-eyed when she was a baby and that her eyes were healed as a toddler. Perhaps that is why she had such great faith at a young age.

She had experienced many answers to her prayers, including one that took place when she was just 7 years old.

While living in Houston, Texas, we visited my husband's sister and brother-in-law, David and Glynda Wesley.

They were pastors in Orlando, but they were temporarily living in an apartment because the church had rented out the parsonage.

Like other children her age, Bethany was smitten with Mickey Mouse and Walt Disney World.

Soon after we returned from our trip to Orlando, she began praying earnestly each night that God would let us move there and have a house with a swimming pool.

Bethany loved to swim and had seen many homes with pools in Florida.

At the time, I was pregnant with Clint and had morning sickness that lasted all day. I was in no shape to move.

I tried every way possible to kindly discourage my daughter from saying a prayer that I believed was not in God's will.

Our church in Houston was just getting ready to enter a new building phase. The congregation was growing and things were going well.

I did not want to leave, but Bethany kept on praying loudly and earnestly each night.

She begged God for a swimming pool and a house by Mickey Mouse where her cousins, Shane and Leah, lived. Every evening, it broke my heart.

When I tried to give reasons why God might not want us to move to Orlando, she ignored them and said she knew God answered prayers and that He could perform miracles. *How could I argue with her?*

One day, David called to say they had been appointed to the mission field and were looking for someone to replace them in Orlando.

Clark and I did not jump at the offer. In fact, we turned it down and didn't tell Bethany that her uncle had asked us about moving.

David phoned again and asked us if we had prayed about it. We said we didn't need to pray. The timing was not right, and we did not feel led to leave.

A few days later, he called again and asked us to at least pray about it before we gave him an answer. My husband and I agreed to pray separately for one day.

At the close of the day, God had told us both the same thing. Clark was supposed to go to the interview in Orlando.

To make sure it was God's will, we decided on *five* things we felt needed to take place during the visit—such as the church board agreeing to additionally cover our Houston medical insurance while I was pregnant—if God wanted us to move there.

All five conditions came to fruition, and we felt at peace about relocating.

To our amazement, when we arrived at the parsonage, we discovered it had a large, lovely swimming pool. I'll never forget Bethany's reaction.

She wasn't even surprised. She simply said it was a lot bigger than she had expected, but then, "God was always doing stuff like that."

When she was about 8 years old, Clark and I were involved in a car accident, and I was seriously injured.

Four years later, the insurance company settled our claim, and we were anticipating a check. Our attorney assured us it normally took 10 days to receive the payment.

However, because the office would be closed several days for Christmas and New Year's, it would probably take a little longer. He had done this for years and *knew* we would not get our money until *after* the holidays.

There were only five days left until Christmas, so we explained our financial situation to the girls.

Bethany, who was 12 at the time, could see by the absence of gifts under the tree, that we needed the money *now*.

A couple days later, I arrived home from work to find her sitting on the front porch. She was jubilant.

She explained she'd had a long talk with God and told Him that we needed the money before Christmas. She said at first she didn't hear anything, but she knew if she prayed and waited long enough, He would answer her.

"God always talks to you, Mom. So I told Him I was going to sit on this porch and listen till He talked to me."

Triumphantly, she announced that after quite awhile, He had finally "spoken" and said He would honor her request to make sure the money arrived on time.

I was dismayed because Christmas was only *three* days away, and our attorney had said the insurance company was mailing the money after New Year's.

I did not want Bethany to be disappointed, or worse yet, think God had lied. I reminded her, again, what the attorney had told me and that perhaps she hadn't heard the Lord correctly.

She was adamant. If God said the money would be here, then the attorney was wrong. Neither Clark nor I could dissuade her.

The very next day, our attorney called. He said he had never received a settlement check so quickly in all his years of practice, but he was holding ours in his hand.

We cashed it and immediately went shopping for gifts for our children. We wrapped them the next day and had them under the tree in time for Christmas the following morning.

Bethany had never doubted. I had seen many miracles in my life but I had believed our attorney. It taught me a lesson about having "childlike faith."

I should have remembered that God is not moved by great people. He is moved by *great faith*!

Chapter 11:

Miracles and Faith

I am often asked, "How did your faith grow strong enough to *hear* God tell you Bethany was going to die the night of the accident?"

My response, "It happened gradually."

Faith begins as a tiny seed, and like any living thing, it must be watered and nourished to grow.

Christ taught if you have faith the size of a mustard seed, you can move mountains.

For many years, I did not accurately understand this concept. It was Tammy, a co-worker of mine, who helped me realize what it meant.

Shortly before Bethany died, I shared with Tammy how frustrated I was about my daughter's drastic change in behavior and her departure from all the spiritual values she had been taught.

"I must not have much faith, Tammy. It seems like no matter how much I pray, *I'm* not moving any mountains."

"You're not supposed to," she said. "*God* is the one who moves mountains. It is *your faith* that *moves God*."

It was like a light bulb went on! I had been praying, "Lord, help *me* reach Bethany. Help *me* save her."

After my conversation with Tammy, I started praying, "God, I believe *You* can reach Bethany. I know *You* can bring her back to her faith."

I had always known that God could perform miracles and could even "speak" to us. It took awhile, however, before I experienced them and heard Him for myself.

My mother often said that God had spoken to her, and I clearly remember the first time I discovered He actually did.

I was 7. My parents and I had driven from Battle Creek, Michigan, to visit my mom's brother, Uncle Harold, and his wife, Aunt Eileen, in Los Angeles, California.

On our way back, we left in the wee hours of the morning to escape the rush hour traffic. Mom and I had fallen asleep, leaving only my dad awake at the wheel.

Suddenly, I heard my mother scream, "CLARENCE!! WATCH OUT!!!"

I woke up to see our car heading straight for the guardrail of an overpass.

My father jerked the 1963 Chevy Impala in the other direction. We swerved back and forth until he got the car under control.

Horrified, Dad realized he had fallen asleep. He asked my mother how she knew what was happening, since she had dozed off. She answered, "A voice yelled 'WAKE UP, FRANCES!! WAKE UP!!' "

At first she thought my dad had called her, but when she opened her eyes and looked at him, she noticed his eyes were closed. She quickly realized the *voice* had been a supernatural warning.

When we arrived home, we spoke to my uncle. He asked if we had experienced any close calls on the highway after leaving his house that morning.

My mother was shocked and said "yes."

Uncle Harold told her that he was heading to work on the busy L.A. freeway around 7:30 a.m. Suddenly he saw a vision of our car demolished, lying at the bottom of an overpass.

Apparently, we had gone over the bridge.

The vision was so vivid that he actually pulled over and prayed fervently for God's protection.

He prayed until he felt a peace that the Lord was going to save us. He then looked at his watch and noted the time.

Uncle Harold and my mother both agreed the voice she heard was God's.

After that, I knew He spoke to His children, but I thought you had to be a saint to hear Him.

My mother spent hours reading her Bible and praying, so I was not surprised that she was worthy of communication with Him.

It was an admonition from my Uncle Harold, in fact, that ultimately led me to my *own* conversation with God.

At age 23, I had already graduated from Greenville College, a Free Methodist school in Illinois.

I had moved to Ocala, Florida, to be near my mother, who was living with her sister, Margaret. My father, at the time, was in a nearby nursing home.

As a young adult, I had an apartment that I shared with a college friend, Jeannie. I was also working as an assistant to the first vice president of a large savings and loan.

I spent a lot of time shopping, dating and going to clubs with friends. I attended church, too, but my walk with God had taken a backseat to all my other activities.

When my father died in May 1981, a year after I finished college, I was devastated.

That Christmas, Uncle Harold visited my mother and aunt for the holidays.

One evening, while I was at my mom's house, I became indignant when my uncle said he was praying that I give up my love of worldly things and seek holiness.

He suggested that I quit my job and attend a Christian graduate school because he *felt* God wanted me to go into ministry.

Irritated, I told him that I was not interested in more schooling, ministry or holiness. Then I barely spoke to him the rest of the day.

Soon after Uncle Harold left, Jeannie was transferred to work in another city, and the young man I had been dating broke up with me and moved away. I was still grieving from my father's death and now felt completely alone.

When I developed a mild case of mononucleosis (a viral infection causing fever, sore throat and swollen lymph glands), I could not work and collapsed both physically and emotionally.

Lying in bed, I cried out angrily to God in my spirit, "WHAT MORE CAN YOU TAKE AWAY?"

"Anything you can hold on to." The voice was calm but firm. It was a thought that was not my own. I froze. It was the first time I had *heard* God reply.

As a child, I had always prayed at bedtime. Growing up, I graduated from "now I lay me down to sleep" to asking God to watch over my loved ones and help me with a test before I collapsed into bed.

I talked *to* God...not *with* Him.

Imagine how shocked I was when He answered me this time. As sick as I was, I called my mother and exclaimed, "Mom, I just heard *God speak!*"

"Good," she answered, "that means you were finally ready to listen."

While I was recuperating, she gave me a book to read by Charles Colson called *Born Again*.

Colson was a member of Nixon's White House administration and was convicted for his role in the Watergate scandal.

In the book, he discusses his prison experience and his consequential work with inmates after being released.[4]

His story inspired me so much that when I recovered, I began volunteering at a nearby school for juvenile inmates. Focusing my time and energy on the girls gave my life meaning.

Later the McPherson School staff presented me with a certificate for outstanding volunteer service.

This experience motivated me to ask my mother if I could attend Bethany Nazarene College to study Christian counseling in the graduate department.

To my surprise, she told me that my father had already set money aside before his death—in case I decided to return to school for counseling, which was my original desire.

Immediately, I remembered the words of Uncle Harold and realized God had gone to drastic lengths to get me on the path *He* had planned for me.

Born Again

In the spring of 1982, I enrolled in the graduate program at Bethany Nazarene College in Bethany, Oklahoma.

During the first chapel service, one of my professors who was also an ordained minister, explained the difference between salvation and sanctification.

Using the analogy of driving a car, he said when we seek salvation and repent, we acknowledge to God that we have been driving in the wrong direction.

Tired of the collisions and accidents our sins have caused, as well as the pain and damage we have done to ourselves and others, we admit we are sinners; apologize to God; and ask for His help to stay on the right road.

In other words, we open the door of our heart and let Him in. As we continue through life, we are able to ask God for direction and He gladly gives it.

However, His presence in our heart never negates our own free will. We can listen to Him or choose not to.

When we seek holiness, we not only want to be forgiven of our sins, we want to be free of our "sinful nature," the *innate desire* to do wrong.

The speaker went on to say that when we are saved, God can tell us to turn right or left (for example, not to date a certain person or wear immodest apparel).

Yet, if we are still controlled by our sinful nature, we will often choose to go straight ahead, doing and wearing what we want.

Ouch! This was a dagger to my conscience!

I had definitely been ignoring God in both areas of dating and modesty. Consequently, I had suffered a broken heart many times by dating men with wrong intentions.

After so many disappointments and heartaches, I was tired of doing things my way. I had made my own decisions and they had led to dead ends. I realized I needed God to "drive my car."

Humbled, I walked to the altar at the end of chapel and asked the Lord to cleanse my thoughts, motives and desires.

Until then, I never wanted to give God complete control of my life. I thought He would force me to do things I didn't want to do or make me give up things I still wanted.

The opposite is true.

After being filled with the Holy Spirit, I put on a favorite outfit but noticed it was extremely tight and had a very low neckline. I used to feel pretty in it—now I felt strangely uncomfortable.

I asked God, "Should I take this off?"

He answered calmly, "It's up to you. Do you want to attract men who like you because of your body or because of who you are? Do you want a man to lust after you or fall in love with you?"

I discovered that God never forced me to do anything. He would simply give advice and leave the decision to me.

The difference was, because His Spirit now lived in me, I no longer wanted to do things *my* way. I preferred to take His advice.

My desires and my entire attitude changed.

Before, I had *served* God but it was with a servant's mentality.

I had done things because I was afraid He would discipline me if I didn't obey. I went to church, read my Bible and prayed "out of duty."

After surrendering that day at the altar, I no longer *served* God. I *worshipped* Him.

I looked forward to church and read my Bible because I longed to spend time with Him and be in His presence.

Instead of kneeling by my bedside and saying a quick prayer, I would lie in bed and talk to Him at length about everything in my life.

When I finally opened my eyes, I would be shocked to discover that 30 minutes had passed.

I talked to God as I drove or walked across campus...any time, anywhere. I finally understood what the Bible meant when it said to *"pray without ceasing"* (I Thessalonians 5:17).

God, in turn, would communicate with me through thoughts and also through sermons and scriptures. Our relationship became personal, and we were intimate friends.

One day, I was feeling discouraged that I still had not met the right man as yet.

As I read the Book of Jeremiah for an Old Testament Literature class, God used Jeremiah 29:11 to speak to me,

For I know the plans I have for you, declares the Lord, plans to prosper you and not to harm you, plans to give you hope and a future.

Later that year, I met my husband on the campus of Bethany Nazarene College and discovered that God did have *the perfect plan* for my life.

The Perfect Plan

Clark and I got married in July 1983 and moved to Kansas City, Missouri, so he could attend seminary.

Being an only child, I had always longed for a family.

In September 1985, our first daughter was born. We named her Bethany, which means *place where God abides,* to remind us of the college where we met.

Arriving two weeks early, she weighed 5½ pounds and was 18" long. Bethany was beautiful, but by 9 months old, she became severely cross-eyed.

Pastor Keith Wright of Kansas City First Church of the Nazarene dedicated her to God when she was born and later prayed for her eyes to be healed.

Despite a delicate eye operation, she still had to wear thick, tri-focal glasses.

However, Bethany's eyes were miraculously healed a year later in Texas, which I will elaborate on shortly.

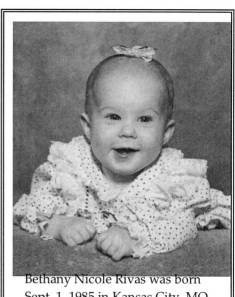

Bethany Nicole Rivas was born Sept. 1, 1985 in Kansas City, MO.

Our second child was born in December 1986. We named her Kristin, a derivative of the word *Christian*, which means *follower of Christ*.

When Kristin was 5 months old, Clark graduated from seminary and was offered a small church in Lufkin, Texas.

Because it was a rural area and only a handful of people, mostly elderly, attended the church, I did not want to live there.

In fact, I told God I would *not* move unless He made it so plain that I could not deny this was of Him. I decided to make demands I thought could not possibly be met.

Knowing that the previous pastor had retired and the church and parsonage were very old, I told God that the house had to have a nursery and playground for Bethany and Kristin.

Then I threw in a few things I wanted, like a large, formal dining room and a family room with a real fireplace.

We flew to Lufkin for a tour of the facilities and quickly learned that the previous owners had recently done a lot of remodeling to the parsonage before they left.

Since they often kept their two small grandchildren, they had turned one of the bedrooms into a nursery and had a sturdy, custom-made play set in the backyard.

The pastor had also added a new wing to the house that included a *large, formal dining room* and a lovely *family room* with a *real fireplace*.

As we boarded the plane, God asked, "Is there anything else, Sharon?"

I simply said, "No, thank You," and began to pack as soon as we returned home.

Prior to leaving Kansas City, we were urged to have a second operation on Bethany's eyes once we moved to Texas.

Even though the surgery would be dangerous, her eyes were so bad that the doctor thought the best chance of ever correcting them was to operate while she was still young.

He recommended a specialist in Houston who worked with the astronauts and said he was the best in the business.

Bethany pushes Kristin in a toy shopping cart.

She plays with her cousin, Shane Wesley.

We drove two hours from Lufkin to Houston, and the doctor agreed that Bethany needed surgery immediately!

However, God intervened and performed a miracle on her eyes as a toddler.

Enclosed is a portion of the letter I wrote to Pastor Wright after Bethany died, letting him know that God had, indeed, answered his prayers.

Dear Pastor Wright:

As you know, the first surgery on Bethany's eyes failed. After moving to Lufkin, Texas, her second surgery was scheduled to take place in an elite hospital in Houston. She was to be operated on by the best eye doctor in the United States, the one who takes care of the astronauts.

On Sunday evening, the night before the surgery, Clark asked the church folks to come forward and once more pray for Bethany's healing.

They hobbled forward and laid hands on her but I confess I thought it was a waste of time since the prayers of our seminary professors and the General Superintendent of our entire denomination had not succeeded.

On Monday morning we arrived bright and early at the hospital. The doctor examined Bethany's eyes for final measurements. Then he measured them again. Next he called in another surgeon to examine her.

Finally he asked, "Have you taken this child to another doctor for surgery?" We said, "No, of course not! You're the best in the world! Where else would we go?"

Puzzled we asked, **"Why do you want to know?"** He replied that Bethany's eyes were completely normal and he could not explain it since she was one of the worst cases he had ever seen in his entire career.

I then asked him, "Sir, do you believe in prayer?" He said not really, that he was more of an atheist. Then I told him about the little elderly group of church people that had anointed her for healing the night before.

Slowly he went back to his desk and sat down. He sat there for quite some time. Then he finally turned on his tape recorder to dictate his medical notes.

After stating that her eyes no longer needed to be corrected he finished by saying, "I have decided to cancel the operation on Bethany Rivas, *a greater physician...than I...has worked on this child.*"

Bethany knew that story well. She could never deny the miraculous healing power of God. I have come to believe this—sometimes God allows us to go through difficult things because He is trying to reach *someone else*.

Bethany was not healed the first time because there was an older doctor in Houston, about ready to retire, who was an atheist and needed to know that God *did* exist.

And I have also learned this...the greatness of the miracle does not depend on the greatness of the title of those praying for it. God has a reason for not healing us...or not healing us *yet*.

He has His own divine plan and **His** ways are higher than *our* ways.

Chapter 12:
Answered Prayers

The healing of Bethany's eyes when she was 2 years old increased my faith tremendously.

Still, there were some things I thought might be too insignificant to pray about. I wasn't sure if faith counted in those areas, but I was wrong.

Bethany and Kristin were inseparable and loved to watch Sesame Street when they were young.

They would sit together, eating their cereal as they giggled and pointed at the puppets, especially Big Bird.

Bethany and Kristin shared a love for Big Bird!

Living in the rural area of Lufkin, we needed cable to get good reception for even the basic channels on our TV.

However, finances were often tight in our first pastorate, and when we had to choose between buying groceries and paying cable, food won.

Since we were two months behind on the cable bill, we received the dreaded letter, stating that our service would be disconnected.

At first, I was embarrassed to ask God for such an insignificant matter as a $63 cable bill, but I decided to petition Him anyway.

Although I didn't tell anyone about our financial need, day after day I went through the mail, hoping a relative would have suddenly decided to be generous.

The deadline was on a Friday at noon, and that morning I prayed especially hard.

When I went to the mailbox, I found a strange envelope with no return address or letter, only a check for $65 from someone whose name I didn't recognize.

It was one thing to receive a donation of $25, $50 or even perhaps $75 from a family member or friend. However, $65 from a stranger with no letter of explanation attached was miraculous.

Even though I had prayed for a week, I was shocked about the check, but I quickly cashed it and paid the bill. Needless to say, the girls were delighted to watch Big Bird that day.

As I saw their joy, I marveled at the graciousness and goodness of God to miraculously provide for something so simple, because He cared about two little girls. I also wondered whom He had used to bless us.

Several months later, when a group of fellow Nazarene pastors and wives from neighboring towns got together for a friendly dinner, I shared my story of the miracle money.

Rev. Brance Moyer, pastor of the larger Nazarene church in town, asked me to repeat the name on the check, as it sounded familiar.

A few days later, he called to tell me that he had solved the mystery.

The check belonged to the parents of one of his church members. They had visited their daughter for Thanksgiving, and she had invited him and his family over for dinner.

When Rev. Moyer was asked how the new pastor of the little Nazarene church in Lufkin was doing, he told them Rev. Rivas was fine and that his own daughter often played with Pastor Clark's two little girls.

Recognizing the name on the check, Rev. Moyer contacted his church member. She confirmed that her mother had indeed called her and asked for the address of the pastor who preached at the other church. She hadn't asked her mother for an explanation at the time but agreed to call her.

It turns out that each morning for a week, God had told her mother to mail a check to Pastor Rivas.

Since she did not know him and he wasn't even her daughter's pastor, she ignored the voice. Still, the thought persisted and grew stronger.

Finally one morning, God told her that if she didn't mail the check that day, the need of the pastor's family would not be met. When she asked the Lord how much to send, He told her $65.

She quickly called her daughter who found our home address in the phone book. The woman then enclosed the check but didn't have time to write a note because the mailman had arrived.

After hearing the story, I was amazed. I wondered why God had asked a total stranger to help us.

The more I thought about it, though, the more I realized that God often answers through ways we could never have imagined. That way we know it is *Him* working and not just coincidence.

If someone had known our need and given us the check or a family member had mailed us some money, we would have simply accepted that as "natural" events.

In the same token, if Bethany's eyes had been healed when dignitary church leaders had prayed for her, we might have been tempted to think it was the power of *their prayers* rather than the power of God.

I finally realized no problem was too small for Him to care about. After the Big Bird lesson, I became an avid believer in miracles and began to understand the phenomenal power of prayer.

My faith grew as I exercised and nourished it with prayer and spending time alone with God and in His Word.

I knew to turn to Him immediately when a need arose, which is what I did several years later.

After leaving Lufkin, we pastored a newly planted church in Richmond, Texas, a suburb of Houston.

To raise money one year for our contribution to an overseas building project, Clark challenged our church members to join him in giving an offering equal to one paycheck per family.

Since I did not work outside the home, I had no idea how we were going to *live* after Clark turned over his entire check for the missions offering.

We had just spent money on car repairs, so we had about $6 left in our bank account.

That night, we had a potluck dinner at church. Although they had never done it before, family after family insisted we take the leftovers home. Our need for food had been met.

The next day, while Clark took the girls inside the library to check out free videos, I vividly remember sitting in the car, praying.

After a few minutes, God interrupted my thoughts and asked, "How much money do you need?" I wasn't sure.

He said, "Write it out and add it up. Tell me *exactly* how much you need."

I still had to buy milk and eggs, along with a tank of gas, and several bills were due. The total amount on the paper was about $100.

When we arrived home, I nearly keeled over. Wedged in the door was a check for $100 from Griff Duty, a gentleman who seldom attended church. I doubted he knew we had donated our entire pay to missions the day before.

I distinctly remembered a conversation I'd had with Griff recently. He and his wife, Julie, had accompanied Clark and me as chaperones on a teen youth retreat.

On the return trip to Richmond, Griff asked me about my relationship with God. He was skeptical to believe that anyone could "hear God's voice" like I said I did.

It had been several months since we had spoken. Yet, to my amazement, there was his signature on the check.

I went inside the house and called Griff. I wanted to thank him and ask why he had left the money. He said he was about to call and ask me the same question.

He explained that he was driving pass our subdivision on his way to work when a thought, which was not his own, popped into his head, "Give Pastor Rivas $100."

Immediately, he wondered if it was God talking to him.

"Yesterday was Sunday, so Pastor Rivas just got paid," Griff promptly responded.

"Besides, my construction jobs are all done, and I only have a *couple* hundred dollars left to live on myself," he continued to rationalize.

"I don't know if I will be awarded any of the bids I've submitted on new jobs, so this money has got to last."

God replied, "I can give you all three bids you quoted if you help Pastor Rivas. Or, I can make sure you get none of them, and you can live on the *$300* you have left."

Griff said he suddenly realized he had not told God it was three bids or that he actually had $300 left in the bank instead of $200.

At that point, he turned his truck around and left the check at our front door.

When he arrived at his office, all three contractors called—a week early—and awarded him the jobs.

The next Sunday, he came to church and gave his life to Christ.

After Clark and I left Texas, Griff and Julie became leaders of the youth group.

Over the years, I have collected journals with pages of miraculous interventions by God.

Although He does answer prayers and meet needs, He is not a "Cosmic Genie" who grants our every wish.

He doesn't just bail us out and mail us checks when we overspend. He often allows us to suffer the consequences of wrong actions or bad decisions.

The night Bethany died, I begged God to save her. He saved her *soul* but not her *life*.

I simply mention these past experiences so you will understand how I knew it was God's voice that woke me up before the accident, and why I was not surprised at the miracles that occurred afterward.

In fact, I believe God also prepared Bethany for that fatal moment because of a Christmas Eve devotional He asked me to share nine weeks earlier.

Christmas Eve

Ever since our children were young, we have read the story of Christ's birth the night before Christmas. After Bethany moved out, she told us that she wanted nothing more to do with God.

Consequently, we didn't expect her to attend the Christmas Eve reading at our home that year.

To our surprise, she called to confirm that she and her boyfriend would be there.

The next day, during my morning devotion, I read a story about Judas betraying Christ and how, instead of repenting when he felt remorse, he hung himself.

In contrast, Peter had denied Christ three times, but when he heard the rooster crow, he felt remorse, wept bitterly and repented.

Both men betrayed Christ; both felt guilt and shame; and both men went to a tree.

Judas chose to go to a tree in the woods and hang himself, and therefore was lost for eternity.

Peter went to the old rugged cross, found forgiveness and became one of the most powerful disciples in the Bible.

The devotional went on to say that if Judas had only realized the Lord would have forgiven him, he would have gone to the *right* tree.

As I closed the book, God clearly whispered, "This is the devotional I want you to give on Christmas Eve."

"What?" I abruptly responded. "We always read the Christmas story about Your birth."

"This one is for Bethany," He replied.

On Christmas Eve, I obeyed and told everyone that God wanted me to share a different devotional this year.

The story, I explained, had nothing to do with Christmas, except that the tree of Christmas eventually becomes the cross of Easter—for Christ was born in a manger solely to die later for our sins—*so we would not have to.*

As I spoke to my family about guilt, repentance and forgiveness, Bethany stared at me uncomfortably. I ended by telling them about a strange event that had occurred a few days before.

When Clark and I pastored the church in Lufkin, there were only two teenagers, David and Elise. We took them under our wings, and they spent a lot of time in our home.

It had been 15 years since I'd heard from Elise.

That year, we received a letter from her, asking us to forgive her for something she'd done as a teen and to please write back.

I immediately responded, letting her know we had forgiven her and were indeed praying for her.

However, I misplaced the envelope with Elise's mailing address, so I could not mail my letter.

It had been six months and as Christmas drew near, I felt an overwhelming burden to contact her.

Since I could not remember her married name or where she'd moved to, the only thing I could think of was to find the other youth member.

David had emailed us while he was in the service, but he had left the military and we had no way to contact him.

Heartbroken, I told my family how I stood at the kitchen sink a few days earlier, washing dishes and praying, "God, please tell David to contact us.

"I know we've moved since the last time he wrote, but You can help him find us again," I petitioned God.

"And please, help him to do it soon. It's only a few days till Christmas and I need to reach Elise."

Exactly 15 minutes later, the phone rang. I dried my hands and picked up the receiver. A man's voice asked, "Is this the Rivas residence?"

"Yes, may I ask who's calling?" (I did not recognize the deep voice on the other end.)

"My name is David Powers," he responded. "Do you remember me, Mrs. Rivas? I was the only teenage boy in the church you and Brother Rivas pastored in Lufkin."

I almost dropped the phone!!! "David," I gasped, "it is so good to hear your voice! Thank you for calling, but I have to ask, *what made you call just now?*"

He simply replied, "You tell me!"

David, a deputy sheriff in Texas, explained that he was driving down the highway when God said, "Call Pastor Rivas."

Since he, too, had lost track of us years ago, he told God, "I don't even know where they live, much less their phone number."

That's when God told him, "David, you're in a patrol car with a computer. Look it up!"

With intentions to search for us as soon as he returned to the station, he heard, "DO IT NOW!"

The command was so forceful that David pulled over and started looking for our number on his computer.

"Is anything wrong, Mrs. Rivas? Why did God tell me to call you?"

Still in shock, I told him about Elise, her letter and why I needed to find her. David did not know her married name either but said he would look for her father's phone number.

In the meantime, he filled me in on his life, his walk with God and his desire to be a good Christian husband and father from seeing Clark's example in our home.

After David gave me the number, I thanked him for calling, hung up and immediately dialed Elise's father to ask him for her address.

While speaking to him, Elise walked through the door. (Now that's precise timing!)

When we heard each other's voice, we both started crying. She said she was feeling depressed because Clark and I hadn't written her back.

Elise thought if she didn't hear from us by Christmas, either her letter hadn't reached us or we hadn't forgiven her. I explained that we had lost her letter but had forgiven her years ago and still loved her.

We had a wonderful conversation, and she thanked me for my friendship to her when she was young.

Before we hung up, she told me she was trying to be a good Christian wife and mother by following the example she had learned from me years ago.

As I finished telling my family the story about David and Elise, I said, "God gave me a wonderful Christmas gift this year. It's more valuable than money, fame or success.

"He had two people tell me that Dad and I made a difference in their life and that one day, we would see them again in heaven."

For some reason, I was led to say, "If I'm ever in a car accident and dying on the side of the road, the only thing that will matter to me is knowing my family will be together in heaven forever.

"And, if any of you are ever in a car accident and lying on the side of the road, remember you don't need a preacher or an altar to get saved. God will forgive you right where you are."

In closing, I added, "No matter what you've done, or how many times, you can still come *Home*. God will be waiting.

"And if you ever need to get a message to someone, tell God. He will deliver it."

Nine weeks later, as Bethany was dying on the side of the road, I believe the Lord may have reminded her of this Christmas Eve devotional.

And in those final moments, she may have asked Him to get a message to us.

He did. He sent us a letter. It was the first of many miraculous ways God comforted me.

Chapter 13:

Sufficient Grace

In the Bible, the apostle Paul asked God repeatedly to remove a thorn that was causing him pain. Instead of removing it, the Lord said, *My grace is sufficient for thee* (2 Corinthians 12:9).

Before a tragedy, you cannot imagine how God could ever give you enough grace to go through it, whether it is a natural disaster, divorce, terminal illness or death. Yet, as many Christians will testify, He *does*.

The healing process is not a chart with a straight line ascending smoothly upward. It is a graph with peaks and valleys.

In the days following Bethany's death, it was hard to get out of bed. Waking to reality used to rescue me from horrible nightmares.

Now, *reality* had become the *nightmare*. My first thought every morning was, *"BETHANY IS DEAD!"*

It seemed unreal, yet the nausea in my stomach started anyway. My pulse would *race* and my heart would *pound*.

Although I could not accept it in my head or my heart, something in my gut knew it was true. I was angry and confused.

I thought, "How could this be happening to *me*?"

One morning, as this question raced through my head, I instinctively reached for the remote control to turn on the TV as a distraction.

I flipped through the channels, looking for anything loud enough to drown out my thoughts.

It only took a few clicks before I heard a man shout, "Have you ever asked yourself, *'How could this be happening to me*? I've always loved God and been a good person. Why would God let this *happen to me?'* "

I stopped instantly. Dr. Zachery Tims of New Destiny Christian Center in Apopka, Florida, was preaching about Job in the Bible. I listened to the rest of his sermon without moving.

Moments like this repeated themselves throughout the next few months.

Some mornings, I would feel okay, but if I woke up angry, Pastor Tims' message would pertain to dealing with anger.

If I woke up extremely depressed, he would discuss the steps to overcoming discouragement.

After listening to his messages each morning, God used Pastor Tims to teach me a valuable lesson a year later.

There had been many requests for the memorial booklet I had compiled after Bethany died.

I felt that God was calling me to write a book and share her story, but I wasn't sure I was ready to start such an endeavor.

I clearly remember the morning when I was in the shower "arguing" about the matter with the Lord.

Although I loved writing and was comfortable speaking, for some reason that morning I was simply too tired to think of doing something new.

Tragedy has a way of changing you. Constant grief ages you, and stress eats away at your insides until you feel hollow.

I used to tell people, "I'm not hard boiled anymore. I'm just a *fragile egg* that could break with the slightest pressure."

The thought of God calling me to take on a huge task or new ministry seemed daunting. At almost 50 years of age, I thought I was simply too old and I told the Lord so.

I remember the conversation with Him distinctly. I also remember what happened as soon as I stepped out of the shower.

The volume on the TV in the master bedroom was turned up quite loud, so I could hear it in our bathroom.

As I started to towel dry my hair, I heard a familiar voice boom out, "Turn to the Book of Numbers and read with me."

Pastor Tims then read the passage of scripture about the 10 spies who told Moses there were giants in the Promised Land and that the children of Israel would never be able to conquer them. Joshua and Caleb attested, on the other hand, that it could be done with God's help.

"Do you know Bible scholars believe Caleb was in his 80s when the children of Israel entered the Promised Land?" asked Pastor Tims.

"Men who were much younger than he had doubts that they could conquer a land full of giants.

"His peers had given up but Caleb had faith. He believed God was able to deliver them. He did not look at his age or his circumstance. *He looked at God*."

By now I had walked into the bedroom and was standing with my hair dripping wet and my mouth hanging open.

Pastor Tims continued, "Has the Lord asked *you* to do something that seems too hard? Has God asked you to start something new but you think you're *too old*?"

"Moses was middle-aged when he saw the burning bush; Abraham was an old man when God promised to make him the father of a great nation; and Sarah was 90 when she conceived Isaac. You are not too old. If God calls you, He will equip you!"

I burst into tears. Once more, God had spoken to me immediately through Pastor Tims. And once again, He was letting me know, *"His grace is sufficient."*

A year later—at one of the most important crossroads of my life and at the precise moment when I had given up on finishing this book—God used Dr. Zachery Tims, once again, to speak to me...this time in person.

He was walking in the doors of the Borders bookstore in Ocoee, Florida, as I was walking out.

In our brief conversation, he said the only words that could have convinced me to keep writing, "I'll be *anxious* to read it when you're done!"

God often used the Bible, my devotional or other inspirational books to minister to me. One of the most outstanding was Pastor Joel Osteen's *Your Best Life Now,* which my friend, John, gave me for Christmas.

I read the book three times after Bethany died. Whatever I was going through, his words spoke directly to my situation.

God also manifested His grace in other ways as well. Sometimes, while waiting in the doctor's office, He would use a magazine laying on the coffee table to encourage me.

Whether the cover article was about a family who had lost a teenager through drunk driving or ways to cope with depression, it was as though the magazine had been placed there, just for me.

It happened many times, but the most astounding was the day after we buried Bethany.

I had been reading *Streams in the Desert*, a 366 daily devotional, which was originally published in 1925.

Now, 80 years later in March 2005, I wondered what any devotional could say that could possibly comfort me.

It is hard to believe, but the following excerpt is for March 11, which I read the morning after my daughter's funeral.

Yesterday you experienced a great sorrow, and now your home seems empty. Your first impulse is to give up and to sit down in despair amid your dashed hopes.... Weeping inconsolably beside a grave will never bring back the treasure of a lost love.... Sorrow causes deep scars, and indelibly writes its story on the suffering heart. We never completely recover from our greatest griefs and are never exactly the same after having passed through them. Yet sorrow that is endured in the right spirit impacts our growth favorably and brings us a greater sense of compassion for others.... God has ordained our truest and richest comfort to be found by pressing on toward the goal. Sitting down and brooding over our sorrow deepens the darkness surrounding us, allowing it to creep into our heart.... But if we will turn from the gloom and remain faithful to the calling of God, the light will shine again and we will grow stronger.[5]

Although J. R. Miller wrote this passage decades ago, God used these words to speak *directly* to me, *Sharon Rivas,* a mother who had just buried her child the day before.

I wept openly at the realization that God cared enough to have this devotion waiting for me.

As I cried, I sensed He was experiencing my grief as well. Because He created us, He knows exactly what we think and can feel exactly what we feel.

The Bible says when Lazarus died, Jesus wept at seeing Mary's grief. He knew Lazarus would live again, but He could feel and experience Mary's emotions.

I can honestly say that morning as I wept, I could *feel* God weeping with me. I knew He felt my pain and was brokenhearted for me.

He let me cry for a while and then He gently whispered, "Sharon, I am *so sorry* for your pain. I know how you feel. My Son died too.

"I felt His pain and I could not bear to watch His agony. Even though I knew He would live again and heaven was waiting for Him, I had to look away.

"Bethany is in heaven with me. She is happy, and you *will* see her again. I know that does not ease your agony right now.

"It will take time for the pain to subside, but I will be with you through it all, and I will use her story to reach others. I promise, her death will not be in vain."

Often, the depression would hit me while driving pass a place that reminded me of Bethany. The tears would start to fall but, instantly, I felt God's presence.

The Lord also consoled me through a Christian station, Z88.3 FM, which I listened to in the car.

Somehow, the DJ would say exactly what I needed to hear…when I needed to hear it.

Sometimes, a 30-second devotional that aired would fit my particular struggle. Although the program was pre-recorded, God knew I would be listening.

Other times, it was simply a song I heard on the radio that met my need. One of the most amazing examples of this was at 1 a.m. during *the storm.*

The Storm

Once, in the middle of the night, I woke up crying from another dream about Bethany. The pain was so bad I could hardly breathe.

To make matters worse, Clark was out of town and it was raining outside. Alone in the darkness with only the howling wind and pouring rain to console me, the agony of my loss was too much to bear.

I cried out, "*GOD, HELP ME! Why am I still in so much pain? Where are you?*" I reached over and turned on my clock radio, which was also set to Z88.3.

When I turned it on, the gentle strains of Casting Crowns' new song, "Praise You in This Storm," were just beginning. I was amazed at how perfectly the words fit my situation.

The lyrics were the cry of someone calling out to God, asking why He had not reached down and wiped their tears away. Yet, they could hear God whisper through the rain, "I'm with you."

The entire song was about experiencing a storm in life, searching for divine strength to carry on and realizing God is the only one who can truly rescue us.

In the end, the singer concludes that though his heart is torn, he will praise God in the storm.[6]

Once more, I wept profusely but this time, they were tears of gratefulness. I realized God *was* listening. I was not alone.

He had heard my cry and answered. Although *my* heart was torn, I would also *praise Him in the storm.*

Chapter 14:

The Blessing

Several weeks after the funeral, I suffered an injury that turned out to be a blessing in disguise.

I had just come home from work and was still wearing high heels. For some reason, I needed to get something on the top shelf of my closet, so I kicked off my shoes and climbed on a chair.

When I jumped down, the center part of my right foot landed squarely on an upturned heel which dug a deep hole into the arch of my foot.

Within minutes, it had swollen and was bleeding profusely. It was so painful, I could not walk on it. The next day, I stayed home in bed.

Halfway into the morning, I was hungry but dreaded hopping down a flight of stairs to the kitchen.

For a fleeting second, I wanted to call Bethany to come and help me. She had always been the little nurse in the family and seemed to enjoy taking care of people.

No matter how young she was, when I was incapacitated, she always stepped up and became the mother—cooking, cleaning and supervising Kristin and Clint.

I had reached for the phone to call her when I suddenly realized she would not answer anymore...that she would *never* help me again.

Like the Tuesday two weeks before, it was another one of those momentary memory lapses that so many people go through following the death of a loved one. I burst into tears.

Grief often came in waves, and that morning, I felt myself drowning in them. The one thing that calmed me during those days was reading my Bible.

Pastor Rick had been preaching a series at church from Matthew 5, so I opened my Bible with the intent of reading that scripture.

Instead, the Bible fell open to the story of Jacob and Esau in Genesis where Jacob received the blessing from Isaac.

I had no intention of reading it initially, but my eyes seemed drawn to the pages.

It was a long story and by the time I finished, I was so hungry, I decided to hop downstairs to make breakfast.

After getting a bowl of cereal, I hobbled to the couch and turned on the TV.

Immediately, the TBN Christian channel came on.

I was about to change it when the minister said, "Today, we're going to study the story of Jacob receiving the blessing in the Book of Genesis."

Suddenly, I knew God was trying to get my attention, so I put down the remote.

The minister preached for 30 minutes on the importance of speaking positive things to our children and "claiming" them for the kingdom of God.

He said we could influence their spiritual life and their future by speaking a blessing over them, either in person or even in a letter.

By the time he finished, I was in the throws of despair. I needed to hear this message four weeks *before* Bethany died instead of four weeks *after*.

If God had gone through all this trouble for me to hear this message today, why hadn't He allowed me to hear it when I could still do something about it and pronounce a blessing over Bethany?

I had no sooner thought the question when the Lord responded, "You did!"

Immediately, He reminded me about what happened on Valentine's Day. I had intended to buy a card and send it to her but I hadn't gotten around to it.

That morning as I started reading my Bible, God interrupted me.

"Today is Valentine's Day and you haven't sent Bethany a card. STOP READING AND WRITE HER A NOTE NOW!"

I was definitely perplexed. I would never have imagined the inner urging of the Holy Spirit telling me to stop reading my Bible. I questioned my thought process and wondered if I was hearing correctly.

"But I haven't finished my devotions yet, and I only have a few minutes before getting ready for work. I can't do both. Shouldn't I read the Bible?" I questioned.

"Besides, I don't have a nice card to write in like the one I wanted to get."

God replied, "It's because you only have a few minutes left that you must stop reading and write a note, telling her you love her."

The feeling again was so strong that I stopped reading and dug through my desk for a blank card and started writing.

I thanked Bethany for all the lovely birthday gifts. Then I told her how much I missed her since she had moved out; how proud I was of her; and how much I loved her.

As I was placing the card in the envelope, the voice said, "Add one more line. Tell her more than getting any gift, your greatest wish is that she and Justin will be with you in heaven someday."

I confess, I said "no."

Bethany had become hostile toward any discussion about God. Talking about religion was making things worse and driving her further from Him, so I had stopped.

I argued this point in my spirit but the answer was firm. "WRITE IT!"

I was actually miffed and told God that the last line would ruin the whole impact of the card.

She would overlook the part where I told her I loved her and focus on the part where she thought I was "preaching" at her again.

Begrudgingly, I added the last line and mailed it early that morning. The next day, Bethany left a beautiful message on our answering machine, which I regrettably erased.

God said, "When you felt 'led' to write the Valentine's Day card and tell her all those positive things—how proud you were of her, how much you loved her and that you wanted her to be with you forever in heaven—you were bestowing 'the blessing.'

"Ever since Bethany cursed you and moved out, she had lived with a subconscious burden of guilt. She never felt completely loved or forgiven, especially by you.

"Clark apologized the day you both met with her at Justin's house. He told Bethany that he forgave her and loved her unconditionally.

"Though he was speaking for both of you, she needed to hear it from you, too.

"The last time Bethany was at your house, I told you to say *I love you*. That was the final barrier to be removed so she would know I loved her unconditionally and would forgive her completely.

"The night she died, she finally understood this and was no longer afraid to come 'Home.'

"She is waiting for you, Sharon, and one day, your wish in the Valentine card will come true. You will be a family again forever!"

I broke down and wept, but this time it was out of joy. I was so glad I had obeyed the Holy Spirit.

We don't always understand *why* God tells us to do something, but there is *always* a reason.

Never Give Up

The first time I learned a lesson in obedience, even though it didn't make sense, was from my mother when I was in 9th grade.

Kay Adams was tall and well-liked, but for some reason, she did not like me. I would go home day after day, telling my mother about comments she had made and things she had done to hurt my feelings.

Mom told me to start praying for her. I obeyed but I confess, Kay was so rude to me that I didn't think my prayer would do any good.

One day, after a fall out with her at school, my mother said, "You know, Sharon, the only way to get rid of your enemies is to make them your friend."

She then challenged me to invite the girl who detested me to a Billy Graham movie that was showing in a school auditorium nearby.

I assured my mother that calling Kay would probably provoke her wrath for me even more, but she insisted I try. So, once again, I obeyed.

Since I was an only child, I was always looking for someone to be my friend. But as lonely as I felt, I had no desire to hang around someone who despised me.

Then my mother said, "The Bible tells us to *love your enemies and pray for those who persecute you*" (Matthew 5:44).

She explained that if we are kind to people who are mean to us, they will eventually be overcome with curiosity and wonder why we are nice to them. If we aren't fighting back, they will eventually stop attacking us.

I knew Kay would be stunned if I called, and I figured she would make a mean remark and hang up. Regardless, I got her number from the phone book and dialed it several times before I had the courage to actually let it ring.

When she answered, I invited her to the movie. There was a long silence on the other end.

To my amazement she said, "Just a minute," and asked her parents if she could go. (She later told me that she was bored and simply wanted to see a *free* movie.)

My parents picked her up and were so sweet that you never would have known how awful Kay had treated me.

The movie, as I recall, was a romance story about a young man who had gone to war and his fiancé prayed for him to get saved.

At the end, there was an altar call for the audience, and Kay was one of the first to go to the front of the school auditorium for prayer.

She asked us right away if we could pick her up Sunday morning for church. We did, and she continued going from then on. Needless to say, we became best friends.

I thank my mother for teaching me such a valuable lesson. It changed my whole outlook on life. I knew God could change any heart, but we have to do our part.

We may have "to go" or "let go." Sometimes, we have to "pick up the phone." We may even have to pray for years, instead of weeks, before the Lord reaches a particular person.

It was this lesson I learned with Kay as a teenager that caused me to *never give up* praying for Bethany. I discovered a few months after her death that I wasn't the only one praying for her.

Chapter 15:

The Story Behind the Cup

Our close friends, Stan and Diane, told us an amazing story about Terri, one of Bethany's regular customers at Starbucks in Clermont.

This Starbucks location had placed a memorial book on the counter for customers to write comments about Bethany.

Although Terri did not sign it, she did speak with me when I called her after the funeral. She was still emotional, but she wanted me to know *her* story.

Terri said she would often stand at the Starbucks counter, looking over the extensive selection of delicious coffees, trying to decide if she would order a new one.

Bethany would wait patiently and then say with a smile, "I guess you're gonna stick with the regular one today, right?"

They would both laugh, and she would bring Terri a cup of black coffee.

"Bethany had such a beautiful smile," Terri told me. "She was always so happy. I enjoyed seeing her in the mornings."

At the time, Terri was attending the First Christian Church of Clermont.

One day when she was at the pastor's home for their Tuesday morning Bible study, a visitor requested prayer for a teenage girl.

The lady explained that she had recently attended a woman's retreat and the speaker, a Mrs. Rivas, had asked them to pray for her daughter who was going through a rebellious time in her life.

Although the girl had been raised in a Christian home, she had recently stopped attending church, left the family and moved in with her boyfriend.

The Bible study members added the young lady to their prayer list, but Terri admitted to me that she didn't pay much attention to the name.

Over the next few months, the group continued to pray for the girl. Then one Tuesday morning, the guest returned to the Bible study with sad news.

The teenager they had been praying for was dead! She was killed Sunday in a car accident.

The woman then asked them to pray for the Rivas family in the loss of their daughter, Bethany. This time, Terri caught the name.

With a sickening feeling, she went home and looked for the news report on the Internet. An article about the crash said Bethany Rivas had worked at Starbucks in Clermont.

Still, Terri could not believe it was *her* Bethany. She drove to the coffee shop and could tell immediately by the look on everyone's face that Bethany was gone.

She saw the memorial book on the counter but could not bring herself to sign it. "There were just no words," she said.

Several months later, she ran into Diane whom she had become friends with while taking community college classes together.

She related the story about the girl who had served her coffee but had died seemingly without God answering any of the prayers on her behalf.

Diane immediately asked Terri if she was talking about Bethany Rivas and told her that she and Stan were good friends with the girl's parents.

She assured Terri that a lady had prayed with Bethany while she was dying. She also told her to please go back and tell the members of her Bible study group that God *did* answer their prayers.

Diane asked if she could give me her phone number, and Terri and I talked for quite awhile.

She said she was amazed to learn how many lives had been touched by Bethany's story since she died.

Before hanging up, she said something I will never forget. "This makes me realize that *everyone* has a story, even the waitress you meet.

"Bethany served me a cup of coffee every morning, and this is the first time I finally knew *the story behind it.*"

Below is an excerpt from the memorial book that many Starbucks' employees and customers signed.

DEAR FAMILY

OUR HEARTS AND PRAYERS
GO OUT TO YOU DURING THIS
TIME OF GREAT SADNESS &
LOSS...
BETHANY SPONSORED LIGHT
AND ENCOURAGEMENT TO
EVERYONE SHE MET (EVEN STRANGERS)
AND THIS MEMORIAL IS A
WITNESS AND TESTIMONY TO THE
LIVES THAT SHE TOUCHED. SHE
PROBABLY NEVER KNEW HOW MUCH
HER SMILE EFFECTED US ALL...
WE WILL NEVER FORGET BETHANY
BUT MORE THAN THAT, I HOPE WE WILL
REMEMBER TO SPREAD LIGHT AND
ENCOURAGE OTHERS TOO! I THINK
SHE WOULD BE PLEASED WITH THAT,
DON'T YOU?

"CHILDREN ARE A HERITAGE FROM
THE LORD AND A REWARD FROM HIM"
PSALMS 127:3
REMEMBER TO SHINE!   RON BROWN

Russia

Six months after Bethany died, I finally turned a corner on my grief. For once, her death was no longer the first thing on my mind when I woke up.

I realized this when my alarm didn't go off one morning, and I only had 45 minutes to get ready for work.

"I've got to jump in the shower fast!" I thought.

The very next second, as my feet touched the floor, I remembered Bethany was gone and reality hit me again.

As strange as it seems, the fact that I had thought of something else first gave me hope.

Still, I often experienced moments of grief.

One evening, I came home from the grocery store in a good mood. But as I was putting away the cheese, it triggered a memory of Bethany and I fell apart.

The wave of depression that rolled over me was so deep that I couldn't even cook.

Clark decided to take me out and asked me where I wanted to go. "Anywhere," I said.

He pulled into the parking lot of a nearby restaurant. As we headed inside, the couple exiting the restaurant *bumped* into us.

We soon realized it was Keith and Jeanine Wilson whom we knew from a former church.

Instantly, Jeanine exclaimed, "Sharon, I was going to call you tonight when we got home! Remember the memorial booklet you sent us a few months ago?"

"It arrived in the mail the night before we left on our mission trip to Russia, so I carried it to read during the flight.

"For weeks, Keith and I had been asking the Lord for guidance as to what to say when we got there. We were supposed to give a testimony but neither of us knew exactly what to say.

"After reading the booklet together on the plane, we realized the one thing we had in common with the Russians was love for our children.

"Our politics, culture and language may be different, but they would relate to the death of a child.

"Since most of Russia is considered atheistic, we thought if we shared the story of how God told you Bethany was going to die and then answered your prayer by sending someone to pray with her, they might believe.

"We had a Russian English teacher translate for us everywhere we went. Before we returned home, God told both of us to leave the booklet with our translator.

"Last night, she emailed us and said her mother had passed away unexpectedly a week after we left.

"She remembered the booklet and decided to read it. She said she was writing to thank us, as it was the one thing that gave her hope.

"Sharon, I was going to call and tell you about it when we got home tonight, but I guess God wanted me to tell you in person."

I was shocked and touched at the same time.

Bethany had often said she wanted to be a youth evangelist and "get others excited about God." I doubt she ever imagined she would take the message to people all over Russia.

I was so excited by the news that the depression completely vanished.

As Clark and I ate dinner, I realized God had us "bump" into Keith and Jeanine for a reason.

He knew losing Bethany had created a hole in our lives that could never be filled, but He wanted us to know her death had not been in vain.

Looking back, I can honestly say that every time I wept, the Lord dried my tears; every time I called out to Him, He answered; and when I could no longer walk, He carried me.

Chapter 16:

Gifts from Heaven

I have heard many stories about people who sensed a deceased loved one checking on them from time to time... until they were strong enough to go on with life.

Other than the mystifying events with our dog that occurred the third Tuesday after Bethany died, nothing else out of the ordinary had happened...until October 2005.

Bethany had always asked for a baby brother, so when we discovered I was pregnant with a little boy, she acted like we were giving him to her.

On many occasions, Kristin would complain that her sister was not taking turns rocking him in the recliner.

After I returned to work, Bethany became like a second mother to Clint, dressing him and making him snacks. She even spanked him once.

Kristin tattled on her as soon as I walked in the door, but Bethany quickly defended her action.

Bethany "adored" Clint!

She said her baby brother had *deliberately* disobeyed her, and she knew we would want her to discipline him so that he would grow up to be a "good, little boy."

Clark and I told her from now on, she needed to tell us when Clint misbehaved, and we would discipline him. Bethany reluctantly agreed.

However, as a big sister, she maintained a "motherly" role in his life, taking him to Sea World and shopping for school clothes. I learned just how deep her affection was after her death.

While picking out her clothes for the funeral, Justin's mother said that Bethany often spoke about Clint and mentioned how much she "adored" him.

Several months later, Bethany's love for Clint would surprise us when he celebrated his birthday—the first one without his big sister.

Since October 5, 2005, fell on a Wednesday, we decided to have his 13th birthday party on Friday, September 30.

When he walked into my room Friday morning, fighting back tears, I immediately asked, "What's wrong, Clint?"

He collapsed dejectedly on the bed and said, "I just realized Bethany isn't going to be at my party."

I walked over and put my arms around him. "I know how much you miss her, Sweetheart. We all do."

He curled up against me and we both cried a little.

Then Clint said hesitantly, "I do miss Bethany a lot, Mom. I think about her all the time. At night, when I'm in bed, I ask God to tell her hello for me."

"But what I meant was, Bethany always gave me a lot of presents. I'm not going to get nearly as many gifts this year."

Bethany celebrates her Sweet 16 birthday with Clint.

After a second, we both started laughing. She was known for lavishing gifts on people for birthdays and Christmas. Bethany would look for sales and hoard items for months in advance.

She always loved parties, and I knew she would hate missing Clint's. But then something amazing happened.

On Sunday morning, Cathy, one of the greeters at church, asked if she could speak to me and Clark after service.

Although we had *never* spoken much before, Cathy began sending postcards to Clint after his sister died.

She pulled us aside and said something unusual occurred two days before, on Friday.

Cathy told us that she was driving in her car, listening to the Christian music station, when the song "Legacy" by Nichole Nordeman came on.

Kristin had sung it recently at a memorial service at our church, so she turned up the radio.

As she was thinking about Bethany, she seemed to sense a "voice" asking her to buy gifts for Clint because this was his "special day."

The thought was so strong that Cathy actually went home and looked in the church directory, which listed each member's birthday.

Since Clint's was on October 5, she was a little confused why she was being led to buy gifts on September 30.

Regardless, Cathy went back to the store to buy some candy and other little things he might like.

Holding a large gift bag, she asked, *"Would Bethany have used the term 'adore' to describe her relationship with Clint?"*

Curious, I asked why she wanted to know. She replied, "The voice I heard said she *adored* him. I thought it was Bethany talking to me but it didn't sound like something a teenage girl would say, so I thought I'd ask you about it."

Immediately, I told her that Justin's mom had said Bethany mentioned how much she adored Clint.

Then Cathy asked, "Why did she say Friday was Clint's special day? Isn't his birthday this coming Wednesday?"

After explaining that we had, indeed, celebrated on Friday, Cathy handed us the bag and said, "Please tell Clint Happy Birthday and that his sister wanted to make sure he had some gifts from her." Clark and I were stunned!

Suddenly, she added, "By the way, it must have been Bethany who wanted me to send all those postcards to Clint.

"I couldn't figure out why I had this overwhelming urge to write notes to a little boy I didn't even know. It was like someone else was writing the words. Now I know who."

Imagine Clint's surprise when I told him the story.

It may be hard to believe that I heard a voice speak to me the night Bethany died. However, since Cathy also confirmed she heard a voice telling her information about Clint that she *could not have known* otherwise, it is hard to deny a supernatural power.

I believe these experiences affirm the existence of life after death and of the Divine.

Three months later, in January 2006, it was this Divine Voice that spoke to me again. It said, "Go home *now!*"

Chapter 17:

Go Home NOW!

In May 2005, Kristin and her boyfriend of three years went on a college mission trip to Africa. While there, they got engaged.

The following months were mixed with joy and sorrow. We were still suffering deeply from the loss of Bethany as we planned the wedding, which was especially hard on Kristin.

Her big sister would have been the maid of honor, so not having Bethany's help and enthusiasm left a hole that was hard to fill.

Kristin had always loved Princess Aurora from the Disney movie "Sleeping Beauty" and over the years, she had collected the figurines.

Now that she was getting married, she scoured the Internet and bridal shops for a gown that was similar to the one Aurora wore.

I distinctly remember the moment she stepped out of the dressing room to show us the one she had chosen.

The sight of Kristin brought tears to our eyes. Not only was she breathtakingly beautiful, but we knew her sister would have wanted to be there with us.

In January 2006, four and a half months before the wedding, Kristin came home from college devastated.

Her fiancé no longer wanted to get married.

Although they'd already had premarital counseling, she told him she was willing to go through more counseling in order to resolve any issues or fears.

They agreed to talk after the weekend.

For some reason, rather than staying in her own room, Kristin quarantined herself in Bethany's bedroom, looking at pictures and old letters.

Gradually, she spiraled into a deep depression.

Although Kristin stayed in bed practically the whole weekend, she struggled with insomnia, which left her exhausted, physically and emotionally.

My heart was very heavy for her as I drove to work on January 24, 2006.

It had only been *10 months* since her sister died. I didn't think she, or any of us, could face another loss so soon.

Because she and her fiancé had been so deeply in love and were both devout Christians, I trusted that they would work through whatever problems they had.

Around 9 a.m., my husband phoned me and said Kristin had called him, sobbing. She had just spoken to her fiancé, and he basically told her the relationship was over.

Clark asked me if I could leave work early to go home and be with her. I assured him I would try.

Since I was responsible for getting the contracts ready for the various construction departments, I felt obligated to complete them before leaving.

There was a huge stack on my desk but I figured if I worked fast enough, maybe I could finish early.

As I began typing, a familiar feeling began to gnaw at me. It was similar to the one I had in the kitchen the Friday before Bethany died.

Only this time, it wasn't telling me to stop cleaning. The admonition was telling me to *stop working and go home*!

With so many people depending on me at work, instead of obeying, I simply sped up. My fingers were flying over the keyboard.

I had promised God I would go home at lunch and check on her, but the feelings grew stronger and more persistent.

A nagging thought kept telling me to "Go Home Now."

To reassure myself that Kristin was okay, I called home. The phone rang quite a few times before a groggy voice answered.

"Kristin," I asked anxiously, "are you okay, Sweetheart? Daddy told me what happened this morning. I'm so sorry. Would you like me to come home early?"

Her mumble was barely audible, "Mm hmm."

"Did I wake you?" I asked. "Were you taking a nap?"

Again she mumbled, "Mm hmm."

I knew when someone was depressed, they often slept to deaden the pain and heartache.

I told her I loved her and to go back to bed…that I would come home as soon as I got all my contracts done.

Kristin hung up without saying good-bye.

Again, I started to type but now the *voice* was emphatic, "GO HOME NOW!"

I was at a crossroad. I wanted to obey but I did not think it would be appropriate for me to leave.

I had only been working a couple hours, and there was a huge contract my boss was waiting on me to complete.

As a *responsible* employee, I always finished my work before requesting personal time off.

I knew my daughter was heartbroken, but what about all the employees in the plant who needed me to finish these contracts?

Suddenly, I heard God speak, not with words, but through a clear and piercing thought.

He said, "You must choose right now which is more important to you—your job or your daughter!"

I sensed something awful would happen if I didn't obey. Immediately, I chose "my daughter" but my stomach was in knots as I thought about what to tell my supervisor, Brian.

I walked into his office and explained that Kristin's fiancé had just broken up with her, and I felt like God was telling me to go home.

He was hesitant and asked if the contracts were done. When I told him "no," he just stared at me.

Reluctantly he said, "Go, I'll handle them!"

On my way out that morning, I shared my ominous feelings with a few co-workers, including the owner's daughter who was about Bethany's age.

Everyone would soon learn that God's warning had, once again, come true.

It took about 30 minutes to get home. When I walked in the door, I called out to Kristin and asked if she wanted to go out for lunch.

She didn't answer, so I figured she was still sleeping. I went upstairs to her room and quietly opened the door but she wasn't in there.

I checked the master bedroom, thinking she may have fallen asleep watching television in our bed. She wasn't in there either.

As I turned to go down the hall, I noticed Bethany's room was in total disarray.

The lid to the trunk where we stored her personal belongings was open and all the mementos, bereavement cards and photo albums were on the floor.

Tissues from two empty Kleenex boxes were scattered everywhere. My heart absolutely broke as I realized Kristin had been sitting in there, missing and needing the big sister she had lost.

Walking down the hallway, I noticed a sheet of notebook paper on the floor outside the bathroom door.

As I drew closer, my heart started pounding and my stomach did a summersault.

On top of the handwritten note was Kristin's diamond engagement ring. I grabbed the letter and, with trembling hands, tried to read it.

Instinctively, I knew what it said but I scanned it anyway. She told us to use the engagement ring to help pay for her funeral. It didn't mean anything to her anymore.

Kristin apologized but said she was in too much pain to think rationally.

She told us to say good-bye to her best friend, Lauren, and her relatives, especially Grandma and Grandpa Rivas, and her Great Grandma Battin.

I skipped to the bottom and read the last lines.

I'm so sorry I couldn't be stronger, Mom and Dad. I thought he would always love me and we were going to be together forever. I can't face losing him after just losing my sister. I just want to go and be with Bethany. Please tell everyone I love them and I will see them on the other side.

I banged frantically on the door and screamed Kristin's name! I tried with all my might to kick it in, thinking adrenalin would give me superhuman strength. It didn't.

I grabbed my cell phone to dial 9-1-1, but my hands were shaking so badly that I was pushing several buttons at once.

Unable to get my fingers steady enough to find the individual buttons, I dropped the phone and raced outside.

My neighbor, Isha, from across the street was sweeping out her garage. I shouted for her to call 9-1-1…that Kristin had left a suicide note and was locked in the bathroom!

She dropped the broom and ran inside to get her phone. Everyone knew we had just buried Bethany.

I continued running down the street, screaming for help.

Suddenly, I noticed a work truck in the driveway a few houses from us. I was shocked because Floyd worked across town and was *never* home this early.

I banged on the door, and he immediately saw my panic. When I told him what happened, he grabbed a screwdriver and raced home with me.

As God would have it, Floyd had been fixing something at his house the night before and had forgotten to put the screwdriver back in his toolbox.

That morning, he had driven home to get it and decided to make a sandwich. It was during those few extra minutes, while he was eating, that I banged on his door.

We rushed upstairs to the hall bathroom, and Floyd immediately began working on the knob. Meanwhile, Isha had dialed 9-1-1 and handed me her phone.

The operator began asking me questions but I was incoherent. I just kept screaming for her to send help.

Within minutes, the police and paramedics arrived. Floyd was taking the screws out of the doorknob plate so they could open it.

"Kick it in!" I yelled, just as the doorknob fell off.

Not knowing what they would find, the police officers tried to hold me back. I pushed pass them and rushed to the bathtub where Kristin was curled up in a fetal position.

Her skin was ashen and her lips were blue. I reached down to hold her but an officer yanked me aside.

The paramedic bending over Kristin exclaimed, "Ma'am, if you want your daughter to live, you have to let us tend to her *immediately!*"

I yelled, "Is she alive?"

They felt for a pulse and found a weak one. A huge knife and empty bottle of pills were lying on the bathroom floor.

Shallow gashes showed Kristin had tried to cut both wrists. Apparently, the knife was too dull, so she had also swallowed at least 20 pain killers, prescribed to be taken once a day.

I realized she must have crawled out of the bathtub to answer the phone when I called, which was why it took her so long to answer. I thought she was napping. Only God knew she was dying.

An officer escorted me downstairs and told me to make any needed calls. Floyd had already phoned my husband, who was petrified.

Clark had just heard one doctor tell him Bethany did not make it. He could not fathom hearing another one say Kristin was gone also.

My husband said it felt like he was reliving a nightmare as he drove home. He could barely speak as he broke the news to his parents and asked them to call others to pray.

Then I called my job and asked Tammy and Kenya, my two Christian friends at work, to also pray.

When the owner's daughter called to check on Kristin, I told her what happened. She immediately said, "I'll be right there, Sharon."

As I recall, she and her mother were the first ones to join me at the hospital. Their presence touched me deeply, and I will never forget their love and support during those critical hours.

Soon, Pastor Rick and his wife arrived, as well as Lauren, who was to be Kristin's maid of honor. Many others followed, including her ex-fiancé and his mom.

Kristin was kept in the critical care unit of the emergency room. The doctors revived her enough to make her drink charcoal, which caused severe and perpetual vomiting.

However, instead of improving, her condition steadily deteriorated.

After several hours, they asked if she had been on any medications. It seemed all their efforts to neutralize the effects of the prescription drugs were not working.

Clark and I remembered that Kristin had been taking a prescription medicine for her skin, which turned out to be complicating the situation.

I believe the doctor told us she only had a 50/50 chance of making it through the night.

Later that evening, an orderly came to the waiting room and somberly motioned us over. Normally, someone just came to us with an update.

This time, he escorted us down a long hallway to a small, private, sitting room and closed the door.

Suddenly, we were reliving the same nightmare we had experienced the night Bethany died.

My legs grew weak and my stomach churned. I could not endure being told we had just lost another daughter. The scene was almost surreal as once more the doctor leaned forward in his chair.

"Mr. and Mrs. Rivas, we need you to sign some forms. It's just a precaution, in case we need to do emergency surgery during the night."

By signing the papers, we were giving the hospital permission to remove Kristin's kidneys and acknowledging that we understood, as a result, she would remain on dialysis the rest of her life.

The thought of Kristin having to live that way was horrible. Yet, the fact that she was even alive was a relief. There was nothing else to do but sign.

Although she was basically unconscious, she could still be roused somewhat. Her eyelids would flicker if we called out to her repeatedly.

The next morning, she was taken to the regular intensive care floor, and Clark and I stayed by her side.

We called the Fischers to tell them what happened to Kristin, only to hear that Candy's mother, Virginia, was also in the hospital with acute leukemia.

It had been in remission for months but had suddenly returned, and her condition was deteriorating rapidly.

Once again, we were going through a crisis together, and neither family felt we could face another death so soon.

That night, Kristin remained virtually unconscious until the nausea overcame her. Then she would cry out in pain and delirium as the gut-wrenching spasms shook her body.

This went on all night long as I struggled to change gown after gown, holding her limp, sweat-soaked body in my arms. She had been throwing up every 30 to 60 minutes since being admitted, and by the second morning, there was blood in her vomit.

The hospital had tried to give her clear liquids, but even chicken broth and water immediately came back up. She was weak and had no will to live.

All I could do was cry out to God to save her. I knew it was wrong for Kristin to try and take her life, but I asked the Lord to have mercy on her.

Wasn't it enough that her sister had died? Now, she had just lost her high school sweetheart a few months before their wedding. *How much agony could a young girl take*?

Before I knew it, Rev. Basil Savoie and Kristin's youth pastor, Rev. Charlie Dawes, entered the room.

They were only there a few minutes before she threw up again. I asked them to lay hands on her and pray that the vomiting would stop.

I could not bear to watch her suffer any longer. I wept as they both laid hands on Kristin and prayed earnestly for God to heal her and stop the nausea.

When they finished praying, I made a point to look at the clock. It had been 53 hours since the hospital had given her the charcoal. After that, Kristin never threw up again.

She was later taken to radiology for X-rays to see what damage had been done to her stomach and esophagus.

The doctors were looking for signs of blood. There were none!

Instead, they saw what appeared to be scar tissue, as if there had been a tear in the lining of her esophagus which was now healed.

Kristin was then taken to another part of the hospital to test her kidneys. Clark and I had been told the day before that they were beginning the steep slope to failure.

After waiting some time, a gray-haired doctor returned, looking perplexed. "Mrs. Rivas," he said, "we have tested Kristin's blood and urine several times.

"Yesterday, we thought we had to remove her kidneys when her proteinuria test came back -6.5. It was the worse case I have ever seen. Even patients with kidney disease usually register around -5.

"Today, however, the tests are repeatedly coming back normal. I've been a doctor for many years but I've *never* seen anything like this. I have no idea how our tests could have been so wrong yesterday."

I wish I'd told him that two pastors prayed for her healing.

As soon as we were back in her room, Kristin announced that she wanted to eat. I told the intensive care nurse who promptly said, "Solid food is out of the question!"

After I pointed out that Kristin had not vomited in hours and the X-rays had not found any bleeding, the nurse looked confused and scurried out to check the medical records.

Thirty minutes later, after all the doctors conferred, they hesitantly agreed to let her have food.

Kristin remembers exactly what she ate for her first meal: lightly battered fish; turnip greens (which she normally would have hated but says tasted delicious); corn bread; and peach cobbler.

Several hours later, she devoured a plate of roast beef with mashed potatoes for dinner. To everyone's amazement, she kept every bit of it down.

You can imagine our relief and joy at seeing her health turn around.

When Kristin's memory finally returned, she was able to tell us a very important fact. As she was slipping into unconsciousness, she prayed for God to forgive her and have mercy on her soul.

She told the Lord she loved Him and just wanted to be with Him in heaven because she could no longer endure the pain here on earth.

This taught our family that only God knows the last thoughts or prayers of a dying person, including those who commit suicide.

Therefore, we should not judge a person by their actions, for only God knows the cry of their heart...and He loves His children unconditionally.

The Road to Recovery

In compliance with the Baker Act, which requires suicide attempt victims to have psychological treatment before being released, Kristin was transferred to the psychiatric unit of Florida Hospital for three days.

This was a difficult time because we could only see her a few minutes each day. However, she received good counseling that helped her begin the healing process and rebuild her self-esteem.

The therapist encouraged her to visualize a new image of herself.

In the past, she had depended on her older sister and boyfriend to help her through life.

Losing them had caused a shroud of darkness to wrap itself around her, like a caterpillar in a cocoon, as she lay close to death for days.

Now, she was emerging with a new identity and freedom, with her own set of wings…as a beautiful butterfly.

Although Kristin had taken a semester off to recuperate and attend counseling, she bravely returned to Southeastern University in September 2006.

On January 24, 2007, on what would have been the anniversary of her death, she invited us to visit her at the university. I was unable to go, but Clark took off from work to support her on such an emotional day.

Since President Mark Rutland was out of town, the speaker for chapel was Pastor Roosevelt Hunter.

Pastor Hunter told the students he felt *led* to address those who had suffered from depression, especially to the point of wanting to take their own life.

He wanted them to know God loved them and there was hope. The passage of scripture he cited was Psalm 118.

As Kristin turned to it, she said her eyes fell on the words from verses 17 and 18 (NIV):

I will not die but live, and will proclaim what the Lord has done. The Lord has chastened me severely, but he has not given me over to death.

Kristin felt as though God was speaking to her directly— as He so often does—through scripture. That message of hope was what she needed.

Although her life was spared, she still struggled from the severe emotional stress.

Eventually, her health deteriorated so badly that she had to drop out of college. For over a year, she became a patient of the Mayo Clinic.

She had seizures that increased until they became a daily threat. She was reduced to wearing a seizure helmet and using a cane and wheelchair.

Through a series of God ordained events, Kristin was, once more, miraculously healed and allowed the opportunity to tell her story around the country.

She studied to become a hypnotherapist and currently lives in Seattle, Washington, where she helps others who are suffering emotionally as she did.

As Terri stated in *The Story Behind the Cup*, "Everyone has a story!" I will let Kristin tell hers…in her own book.

Several years after Kristin moved out, I found a letter in her room that she had written to God a month after her suicide attempt. It immediately confirmed the title of this book.

The following is a portion of that letter.

God, I know now that no matter what happens, your hand is on my life and you love me just the same. I will be blessed when I honor your will, even when I can't see it at the time.

No one else had been as good to me as you have and you are never going to change. You will continue to always be there for me.

I may *walk through the fire* with you but I will not be burned by Satan and any tool he may use against me because I have a Spirit of power, and of love, and of a sound mind within me.

You are the breath in my body, so when I can't feel or see you again, with your help, I promise to just breathe your name and trust in you that all will be well.

Guide me down the path that is right. I want nothing but your will alone to be done. Purify me and help me to worship you.

Help me to *forgive* so that *I can be forgiven.*

Chapter 18:

Forgiveness

Like Kristin did in the weeks following her suicide attempt, I would also confront the issue of forgiveness.

After Bethany's death, I struggled with a whirlwind of emotions.

Although I did not hate Steven Michael Johnson, the driver arrested for her death, I was so angry that I could hardly stand to see his picture in the newspaper.

He had a long history of breaking the law and had been let go, let off or let out again and again.

I actually heard an officer who complained about Steven's record say, "We just knew he was going to kill someone sooner or later."

That *someone* turned out to be *my daughter*!

I think most people would understand a parent's anger at losing a child due to the irresponsibility of someone else.

Many people would also understand that they, too, would struggle with forgiving the perpetrator.

I can honestly say that, although Clark and I were angry at the system and hated the fact that we were suffering for its failure, we never hated Steven.

However, it was easier for me to *forgive* because of the experience I had years ago from reading *Born Again* by Charles Colson.

Now, a providential incident would lead me to yet another one of his books.

It was a Wednesday night. As I waited for Clint to get out of his youth group meeting, I wandered into our church's reading room and started browsing the titles.

Suddenly, I noticed Colson's inspirational memoir *Against the Night*. When I picked it up, a flood of memories from his other book came rushing back, and with them came a flood of tears.

I finally understood why the Lord wanted me to read *Born Again* years ago and why He allowed me to work at the juvenile center.

Now I realized I could still have a prison ministry, even if it was to only *one* inmate.

Perhaps, everything in my past had been preparing me for this crisis in my life…to *forgive* the man responsible for my daughter's death.

The next week, I wrote Steven a letter and enclosed Bethany's memorial booklet. I told him I was praying for him because I knew these days were difficult for him as well.

I had no idea of the impact my words or the booklet would have on him.

The Trial

The trial began in April 2007. I had been anxiously waiting for that day, yet also dreading it.

I wanted to see justice done but I was not looking forward to the emotional strain I knew we would endure.

From the beginning, Steven claimed Bethany's boyfriend had been driving. Yet, evidence to the contrary seemed insurmountable.

Although it was Justin's car, a young man at the party attested in a police report that he saw Justin in the backseat when he opened the door to tell Crystal to get out.

Tests also proved the defendant's blood was on the driver-side airbag, and a police report confirmed that Justin had been cut out of the backseat with the Jaws of Life.

To me, it seemed like an open and shut case. By the end of the first day, however, I quickly realized how badly we had underestimated the defense.

During the first day of the trial, Steven's attorneys inferred that it was too dark to clearly identify who was sitting behind the wheel.

They also claimed that Justin could have crawled to the backseat after the initial impact.

While they acknowledged the blood found on the airbag was Steven's, his attorneys argued that he had been ejected from the back, and the impact had caused his nose to bleed.

The blood, they claimed, had dripped from his nose onto the airbag when he leaned in the front window to check on Justin. However, none of Justin's blood was on the airbag.

The second day was the most difficult for me.

When Dr. Jan Garavaglia, known as "Dr. G," testified about the severity of Bethany's injuries, it was, again, one of the most surreal moments of my life.

On her television show, "Dr. G: Medical Examiner," she uses autopsy findings to determine the cause of death for someone in unusual or unknown circumstances.

Since her program was filmed in Orlando, Clark and I watched it sometimes, out of curiosity.

As I sat in the courtroom, listening to the same person I had seen on TV talking about corpses—but now talking about *my daughter*—I felt like I was having a bad dream.

How could she be discussing the "findings" of an autopsy on *our* sweet Bethany? Yet every time she said the words, "The deceased, Bethany Rivas," they would jar me back to reality.

This was no television show. This was *my child* who had been on her cutting table.

It was very difficult to listen to her, but there was one thing she said that did help me.

Contradictory to the police report which stated Bethany was not wearing her seat belt because it was still in a recoiled position, Dr. G reported otherwise.

Since there was a 2-inch wide line of bruising across Bethany's abdomen and her right collar bone was broken, this indicated that she *did* have it on.

For two years, I was angry at her for not "buckling up," thinking if she had, she might still be alive.

Now, learning that the seat belt came apart so easily without tearing the fabric or twisting the metal—as it usually does when it breaks—I realized something rare had occurred.

Once more, it was difficult to assimilate, even painful, but I had to see it through God's eyes. He does not *cause* evil or want us to make bad decisions.

He gave Bethany three chances to save herself: Justin's mother told them to be home by 10 p.m.; her friends warned her not to get in the car; and Crystal's friend told them to get out.

Bethany chose to get in the car and, for some reason, God chose not to keep the seat belt from failing.

The night she died, the Lord asked me if I was willing to allow Him to do "whatever it took to bring her back to Him, including suffering and death."

According to the time on the accident report, the car did not crash until after I said "yes."

I believe God did everything He could to prevent her from being in that car. But when it started down that road, it was too late for her to get out, so He woke me up and asked me to *release* her soul to Him.

God is not cruel. He simply sees things from an *eternal* perspective. He knows what is *truly* important, so His priorities are different than ours. He is much more interested in saving our *soul*…than saving our life.

Dr. G's autopsy result about the seat belt was one of the first pieces of evidence that shed real light on our case.

Steven claimed he was thrown from the backseat like Bethany. However, medical reports showed he had only suffered a broken nose and concussion, and he was walking around when police arrived.

In contrast, my daughter had broken almost every major bone in her body. She also had a cracked skull and was hemorrhaging from her femoral arteries.

The differences were obvious. It seemed much more likely that Steven had been cushioned by an airbag while in the driver's seat.

Yet he calmly and sincerely denied driving and testified under oath that he was sitting in the backseat next to Bethany.

Since I had never been on a jury, I suddenly understood why it was so vital to look at the evidence and not just listen to someone's story.

Toward the end of the trial, the police officer who was first on the scene testified that Steven was kneeling over a body in the road when he arrived.

The officer heard him say, "I think I've killed my friend. I shouldn't have been driving!"

I hope Steven was honestly trying to help Bethany, and his attention to her wasn't merely from fear of her death.

Unfortunately, his cell phone records indicate that he made 13 calls to friends and family after the crash but none to 9-1-1.

This glaring lack of concern for the victims made all of our families furious and did not sit well with the jury, I'm sure.

The officer also confirmed what Donna Weinheimer had written in her letter. He said he checked the vital signs of the female lying in the road and verified she was dead.

However, he clearly remembers a lady giving Bethany CPR shortly afterward and that a Life Flight helicopter was called because she started breathing again.

Hearing him say that my daughter was dead when he checked her made my stomach clinch. However, it gave me peace knowing God had sent someone to revive her and pray with her, just as He promised.

When the defense rested, 25-30 family and friends of Bethany and Crystal were escorted into a private waiting room. Everyone was nervous and on edge, as we waited anxiously for the jury to return.

Suddenly, the entire mood changed, and it was because of Kevin Fischer, Crystal's dad.

After the violent death of a child, it is easy to want revenge. Although Candy and I cried often and experienced depression, Kevin's grief gave way to anger.

He followed the investigation closely, called the attorneys frequently and was determined that Steven would not get away with murder.

Over the months, though, we saw a gradual change as our families talked and prayed together. Yet, I was not prepared for what happened in the waiting room.

At a time when I thought Kevin would be the most adamant for a guilty verdict, he asked us all to join hands. He urged us to pray that God would be in control of the jury's decision and we would have the right attitude, regardless of the verdict.

I simultaneously had to keep my jaw from dropping open and tears from rolling down my cheeks. Clark and I hadn't even thought to pray!

Kevin's attitude at that critical moment proved God is able to give us the peace and forgiveness He supplies—if we will accept it.

When we heard the jury had returned, I was on pins and needles. If the decision was "not guilty," I hoped that God would help us handle it.

To our relief, justice was done. Steven Michael Johnson was pronounced guilty, and sentencing was set for 30 days later.

Out of the Blue

Now that the trial was over, I requested permission to contact Donna Weinheimer, the lady who had been with Bethany until her last breath. I had always wanted to know the details of the night my daughter died.

After receiving Donna's address, I mailed her a portion of the memorial booklet and enclosed a note, thanking her for being the answer to my prayer.

I told her she had helped save Bethany's *soul*, even if she hadn't been able to save her life.

Donna replied in an email how much my note had helped her overcome the guilt she had experienced.

After years of studying how to heal people, she had regretted not being able to *save* Bethany.

Now, she knew she had not failed God or Bethany, and the Lord was still using her as a conduit to minister to others.

Shortly after our email correspondence, Clark and I were able to meet Donna and her husband, Pete. We learned that she was a licensed massage therapist, and she had studied many forms of healing and holistic medicine.

Her desire to serve God had led her to become an ordained minister while incorporating counseling, healing and teaching into her work.

Seeking closure, Clark asked her about that fatal night, and she began to relate the missing details.

Sunday evening, March 6, 2005, Donna was sitting on the porch talking with her friend, Myrna, an out of town guest.

It was around 11 p.m. Normally, she would have been asleep, but for some reason, she felt *compelled* to stay up.

Suddenly, the women heard a crash. Without hesitation, they jumped in Donna's truck and drove about 200 yards to the accident site.

Realizing that Crystal had passed away, Myrna stayed with Justin who was crushed in the backseat, while Donna attended to Bethany who was lying on the road, barely alive.

Since Steven had given them the girls' names, Donna began talking to Bethany, telling her to hang on.

She straightened our daughter's twisted limbs to make her comfortable and laid a coat over her to keep her warm.

It's hard to measure time in that type of situation, she said, but after what seemed like a few minutes, Bethany's heart and breathing stopped.

A police officer who arrived on the scene checked and verified she was dead. Donna immediately administered CPR and continued for several minutes, but Bethany did not respond.

Knowing that brain damage would set in after a long time without oxygen, Donna became desperate and screamed, "COME BACK! DON'T LEAVE, BETHANY! STAY HERE!"

Suddenly, our daughter gasped for breath and her heart began beating erratically, as though she had fought to come back. Donna reassured her that help was on the way.

Over the next few minutes, she believes Bethany was aware of what was happening but struggling to hold on. It was then that Donna prayed with her.

When Clark asked her what she prayed, she told us that she had received the gift of the Holy Spirit and tongues years ago. Therefore, she prayed over her using these gifts.

The Bible says when we do not know how we ought to pray, the Holy Spirit will intercede for us (Romans 8:26).

While Donna was praying, Bethany's breathing, pulse and heart rate became steady and calm.

She clearly sensed in her spirit that our daughter had made peace with the Father and wanted to go Home.

So later, when Bethany slipped away again, Donna said she did not try to revive her.

Hearing this first-hand account of March 6, 2005, was difficult but extremely helpful.

We had always hoped in our hearts that Bethany knew someone was praying with her.

To hear Donna say she believed Bethany did, was very important to us.

At the close of the evening, we hugged and agreed to keep in touch. I'm sure Bethany would be happy to know we are friends.

It's only befitting that the name of Donna's healing and massage therapy school is called "Out of the Blue."

She came *out of the blue,* so to speak, to help my daughter, and later, she was there to give Clark and me the peace we needed to move on.

The Sentencing

Steven Michael Johnson was scheduled to be sentenced four weeks after the trial. Each member of our family was allowed to give a brief statement to the judge.

I read a letter I had written days before, and I broke down at the part that said *my husband would never walk Bethany down the aisle.* When I was finished, Clark, Kristin and members of the Fischer family spoke.

We were all struggling with a lot of anger, pain and resentment. After we were done, the defendant's family addressed the judge.

Believing that, indeed, Steven had not been driving, his girlfriend begged for leniency since their son would never see his father if he was in prison.

I could not help but feel her pain as well.

Before the sentencing, Clint had said he did not want to address the court.

Now, after we were all done and the judge was about to pronounce the sentence, he asked Clark and I if he could say something. We were taken completely by surprise.

Clint had been rather stoic about the trial and continued to remain so as he listened to the statements.

Whatever he wanted to say was obviously important to him or he would not have asked now. The judge allowed my 14-year-old son to approach the podium.

You could have heard a pin drop as he began:

"I hadn't planned to speak, but it seems like there is a lot of anger in the room today," said Clint. "I want Steven to know that I do not hate him. I have forgiven him, and I know Bethany has, too."

"She is in heaven right now and she does not care what is going on down here. She would want us to forgive him. I just want Steven to know God loves him and so do I."

Then Clint quietly returned to his seat. He spoke only a few words, but they had certainly impacted the defendant.

Steven suddenly began weeping and asked his attorney if he could say something. When the judge agreed, he turned around to face his family and friends.

With tears streaming down his face, he finally confessed to driving the car and apologized for what he had done.

He then turned to us and asked our families to forgive him. He said he thought about Bethany and Crystal every day, and wished he had been the one killed that night.

Steven told the judge if he would grant him probation, he would spend the rest of his life trying to prevent others from making the same mistake.

Because he showed no emotion while anyone else had spoken previously, I believe Clint's words affected him.

Whether or not his confession was completely sincere or part of it was to gain sympathy from the court, only God and Steven know.

The judge commended him for admitting the truth and apologizing for his actions. However, he still had to be held accountable for the two lives he had taken and the laws he had broken.

The judge then sentenced him to 35 years in prison.

While we felt relief, Steven's mother wept. I understood her pain because, in a way, she had lost her son, too.

Yet, as Candy pointed out to me later, his mother can see and talk to her child whenever she visits the prison. We will *never* have that opportunity when we visit the cemetery.

Bethany is buried at the back of Woodlawn Cemetery in Gotha, FL, near the mausoleum with a mosaic of Christ.

Visitors are welcome to leave messages in her journal at the gravesite.

Chapter 19:

MADD

After the sentencing, I spoke to Ann Adams, the director for Mothers Against Drunk Driving (MADD) in Lake County where the accident occurred and the trial was held.

Since I lived in Orlando, she referred me to the director in Orange County named Yolanda Larson.

A few days later, I called Yolanda and she invited me to the next victim impact statement class.

Drivers who have had their license revoked for DUI must attend and listen to families of drunk-driving victims tell how their lives have changed.

When I arrived at the Highway Patrol Office where the class was held, I observed a woman named Joyce talk about her son's death. Her story was powerful and gripping.

You could still hear the grief in this mother's voice, even though her child had been killed 12 years ago.

I realized that time never completely heals the wound of a death but neither does it erode the power of the message.

Soon, I began sharing Bethany's story alongside Joyce. Before each class, I noticed that people often entered the room looking very disgruntled.

However, by the time we finished speaking, tears were running down many of their faces.

Yolanda would then ask them to tell us how our impact statements affected them. Their responses usually showed great remorse for our loss and for what they had done.

Sometimes, they were so emotionally overcome that they could not finish speaking.

This happened one night with two teenagers. I distinctly remember them because they looked angrier than most of the faces I had seen.

It was clear neither of the teens wanted to be there. The young man had his arms folded across his chest, and the girl looked completely disinterested. I wondered if I would be able to get through to them.

To my amazement, both had tears running down their face immediately. He was using his shirtsleeve and she was going through a pack of Kleenex from her purse.

When Yolanda opened the floor for comments, they asked if they could talk to me in private.

Lo and behold, they had attended high school with Bethany and knew her very well.

It had been several years since graduation, so they had no idea she had died.

"I didn't want to come here tonight," the young man admitted. "I wasn't going to listen to anything you said until you held up the book with Bethany's picture.

"I used to sit behind her in history class. She was one of my best friends. I can't believe she's dead. I swear to you, Mrs. Rivas, I will never drink and drive again!"

Interactions like this happened at every drunk-driving class.

Whether the attendees were grandparents, housewives or businessmen, they said Bethany's story had touched them, and they promised me that she had not died in vain.

On another occasion, MADD sent me to a middle school in Orange County to talk to approximately 20 students.

Their teacher requested a speaker because they had read a book about a young man killed in a drunk-driving crash.

When I arrived, I learned that we were meeting in the auditorium instead of the classroom because other teachers wanted their students to hear Bethany's story as well.

Row after row of students and teachers filed in until the auditorium was full.

After some quick maneuvering, I was handed a microphone and took the stage in front of several hundred middle schoolers.

As I looked over the crowd, I realized I was in for a challenge. Paper wads were flying, and the students seemed to be more interested in having fun rather than paying attention to me.

The reading teacher asked several times for them to show respect for the speaker but to no avail.

She then took the microphone from me and began belting out "The Star- Spangled Banner" in the most off-key notes.

It was so awful that the students stopped throwing paper wads and held their ears.

"I'll keep on singing until you get quiet!" she shouted and kept right on singing. They began booing in protest, and I nearly covered my ears as well.

"Do you want me to stop?" she yelled. They all nodded and she quickly handed me the mike.

"Good luck," she said.

Needless to say, there was a knot in my stomach. I had about 10 seconds to decide how to reach this mass of uncontrollable bodies, squirming in their seats.

Originally, I was going to introduce myself as a MADD representative but realized I would lose them by the end of the first sentence.

As panic welled up inside me, I prayed, "Lord, help me reach them."

Instantly, I remembered an Allstate commercial that had been playing constantly on TV.

"How many of you have seen the commercial with a group of teenagers in a car, driving down a lonely road while one teen stares out the rear window as the car slowly disappears?"

Almost every hand in the auditorium went up, as I hoped. I told the captive audience that the narrator in the commercial tells us, "Every year 6,000 teenagers get into a car and *they never come home.*"

Then I asked, "How many of you know someone who got in a car and *never* came home?"

To my amazement, almost all the hands went up again. Suddenly, I realized they could relate to my pain.

"My *daughter* is one of those teenagers," I said, raising my photo album with Bethany's radiant smile on the cover.

Bethany and her cat, Gracie.

In her arms was Gracie, her beloved orange and black tiger cat, which she picked out from the Humane Society on September 11, 2001.

There were audible gasps, then silence.

As I told her story, you could hear a pin drop. Every eye was glued to my notebook as I turned the pages of pictures.

Soon, many of the students and teachers were crying. I could see girls opening their purses and handing tissues to their friends.

Several of them, in particular, were weeping profusely.

When I was done speaking, throngs of students from the back of the auditorium crowded the stage for a closer look at Bethany's pictures.

A few of them even asked where my daughter was buried so they could visit her grave.

As I was leaving the school, the reading teacher asked me if I had a moment to chat.

On our way to her portable, she told me that my opening remarks had really hit the students hard.

One of their peers had just been killed in an accident and the funeral had been three days ago. I knew then why God had brought the commercial to my remembrance.

Soon, I discovered the real reason why the teacher wanted to talk to me.

She was going through a difficult situation in her personal life and had been praying—if there was a God, He would send someone to help her.

"Then you showed up this morning," she said. "I believe *you* are the answer to my prayer."

We spent the rest of her grading period talking before we hugged good-bye.

As I pulled out of the school's parking lot, I was amazed at the way God works and how He answers the prayers of anyone who seeks Him.

Although I had not expected to speak to a large audience, I have found that the size of the crowd does not make me nervous, as long as I am prepared.

There was one occasion, however, when I ended up speaking with no preparation at all.

It was September 2008. Clark and I had been invited to an annual awards banquet for the police and prosecutors who worked in the seven-county area of the Central Florida division of MADD.

When we arrived, Yolanda hurried over and told us that one of the main speakers was having car trouble. She asked me if I would speak in her place.

Since I didn't bring the album with Bethany's pictures, I said I didn't think I could.

Clark promptly interjected, "Yes she can!" Then he turned to me and said, "You can do it!"

It was the only time I was *really* nervous. There were about 150 people at the banquet, and I hadn't even *thought* about what I would say. I did a lot of quick praying and thinking—in that order.

In Psalm 81:10, God says, *"Open thy mouth wide, and I will fill it."* That is exactly what happened.

As soon as I stood up to speak, I was no longer nervous.

I briefly told Bethany's story but felt led to mostly thank the police officers for all their hard work and long hours they put in at sobriety check points.

"I had often heard of parents who had lost a child to a drunk driver and my heart always went out to them," I said, "but I never thought I would be one of them.

"I now tell everyone I know to support MADD because the child they save may be their own!"

At the end of the event, a staff member asked me if I recognized the photo on the plaque that was presented to Keith Landry, the Master of Ceremonies and a weekend news anchor at a local TV station.

She said the committee had unanimously chosen the picture because it was so "compelling." Yet, they did not know the name of the young lady in it.

She thought I might recognize her since I often worked at the sobriety check-points where it was taken.

To my surprise, it was a snapshot of Kristin holding her sister's prom picture. It was amazing, especially since I had just told Bethany's story.

This was another occasion when I wondered if it was truly a coincidence...*or providence.*

In loving memory
of Bethany Rivas

Mothers **A**gainst **D**runk **D**riving of Central Florida hosted its annual Law Enforcement Recognition Dinner on September 16, 2008.

A photo of Kristin Rivas holding Bethany's prom picture was on a plaque given to Keith Landry and police officers who were head of their departments in DUI arrests.

Three years later, Mothers Against Drunk Driving created an award to acknowledge the impact Bethany's story had made in the Central Florida area, particularly on drunk-driving arrests.

The "Bethany Rivas Memorial Award" was presented to us on October 19, 2011.

Clark and I then presented the award that night to the Winter Garden Police Department for its 65% increase in DUI arrests made in 2010.

(shown left to right): Travis Waters; Bill Bartko; Nathan Murch; former MADD President Glynn Birch; Clark and Sharon Rivas; Jorge Coello; Mike Mason; MADD Founder Candace Lightner; and Bill Sullivan.

I also had the privilege of speaking about drunk driving at West Orange High, the same school my children attended in Winter Garden, FL.

The following are two letters I received from students in Ms. Iannuzzi's class:

Tiffany Rodriguez
November 17, 2011
Period-6th

Mrs. Rivas,

I remembered everything you spoke about, what you said did not go in vain. I want to thank you for having give your daughters life story to us. I know it is not easy to deal with, trust me, I know that feeling. I never heard such a touching story before. I just wanted to thank you for spending time at West Orange High, and for letting us know that everyone has a life. We need to take care of our lives, because if we dont, then we will be hurting our friends and family, by loosing our lives on Earth. You gave me a wake up call. I will never drink and drive. Your words are wise and sacred.

Sincerely, Tiffany.

11/17/11

Dear Mrs. Rivas,

Thank you so much for taking time out of your schedule to talk to our class about your story. I know it must be hard to share something so personal and it must bring bad memories. I, for one commend you tremendously. You are a very strong women who to your daughters death positively and decided to make a change in the community. This story specifically also touched me because I too, have a sister who is 15 months apart from me and we are so close. It was as if you were describing our relationship. Of course your experience taught me to never drink and drive but to also not take life for granted. I hope you continue to help and prevent drinking and driving. Again thank you for sharing an amazing story. Bethany sounded like a beautiful person and will never be forgotten.

♡ Love,
Alexis Whittaker

Bethany and Kristin graduated
together in May 2004.

178

Chapter 20:

Why Me?

I have wept and I have been angry, but I have never asked God *why* Bethany died. I've lived long enough to know that bad things happen to good people.

Thousands of people die on highways every day. In fact, the National Highway Traffic Safety Administration reports motor vehicle crashes are the number one cause of death for teenagers.[7]

What I want to know is *why* was I given this testimony, and *why* have I felt compelled to pass it on?

For some reason, in the most unusual places—like standing in line at a store, talking to a clerk, sitting beside a stranger at a seminar, anywhere at all—God allows me the opportunity to share Bethany's amazing story.

A few weeks prior to our trip, I fell down the steps at a restaurant and injured my sciatic nerve.

Since I was having a lot of back pain, I went to see a massage therapist while in New Mexico.

As I lay face down on the table in the darkened room, I listened to the soft music and enjoyed the soothing aroma of exotic oils wafting through the air.

I was struggling to stay awake when God whispered, "You should witness to the massage therapist."

"No! No! No!" I moaned in my spirit. "I'm too tired. I'm in too much pain. This isn't the right atmosphere. It's quiet. It's not meant for chit chatting. I don't want to talk about something sad right now. Please don't make me."

There was silence in my spirit as though God was patiently waiting. He does that sometimes, like the night Bethany died.

God simply waits patiently for me to accept His will. The "silence" soon became "heaviness."

When I could bare it no longer, I quietly prayed, "Alright God, I'll talk to him, but *only* if the man specifically asks *what I do for a living*."

I had quit my job shortly before the trial began. Since then, all I had been doing was working on this book.

The therapist had hardly said a word so far, except when he asked, "Where's the pain?"

Now, 20 minutes later—out of the clear blue—he asked, *"What do you do for a living*?"

Still not in the mood to talk, I simply said, "I'm writing a book."

That was it. I didn't volunteer any more information.

Of course his next question was, *"What is it about*?"

"My daughter's death," I answered.

Then he asked how she died, and that's when the whole story came out...miracles and all.

After listening intently, the young man said, *"It was meant to be! You are supposed to write your book."*

He also asked for a memorial booklet, which I mailed once I returned home. Incidences like this happen repeatedly.

One day, I was replacing a cell phone I had purchased only days earlier. The salesman asked, "What's *wrong with the one you just bought*?"

I explained that it dropped calls several times while I was talking to my attorney and editor, which was unacceptable.

Looking surprised, the preppy young man "suggested" that I must be important to have *an attorney* and *an editor*.

When I told him about the book and some of the miracles surrounding my daughter's death, he said, "God must have sent you into the store!"

Then he showed me a text message he had just received a few days before about the death of a good friend.

"You're not going to believe this," he said. "I was lying in bed last night, wondering if there was a God, and if there was, I asked Him to please let me know."

The salesman said that hearing Bethany's story not only answered his question, but it also gave him hope.

He then asked for a memorial booklet, which I grabbed from the car.

After so many "divine appointments," I may have discovered an answer to the question I asked after my daughter's death, "*Why me?*"

Perhaps the Lord allows trials and tribulations to come into our lives so that we can help others, but we must *choose* to do so.

All of us have a decision to make when we experience any kind of grief or loss. We can get bitter and desire pity. Or, we can let Him heal and empower us.

Tragedy has a way of shattering our lives. Yet, if we *allow* God to pick up the pieces, He will arrange them into a beautiful mosaic of new hopes and dreams, and use our story to *reach the world* for Him.

Reaching the World

One of Bethany's goals was to witness to others abroad. Shortly after renewing her faith at a teen summer camp when she was 17, she burst into the kitchen very excited.

She said she wanted to enroll in a program called YWAM (Youth With A Mission) after high school, so she could learn how to become a missionary instead of going to college.

Then she asked me what I thought. To my shame and regret, I did not return her enthusiasm.

I nonchalantly asked her to help me set the table before telling her all the reasons why I thought college would be a better lifelong choice.

"Maybe you could be a *part-time* youth evangelist, talking to troubled teens during summer camps."

I confess. I just couldn't see her sharing the gospel all over the world.

"People who travel internationally usually have an amazing story to tell. What would you talk about, Bethany?"

I probed. "What *amazing story* do you have to tell that would make anyone want to listen to you?"

Instantly, she stopped setting the table and threw down the silverware.

With a look of hurt and anger, she shot back, "I thought at least *you* would support me, Mom! You don't believe in me either, *do you*? You just don't think I can be a missionary!"

Bethany ran upstairs to her room and slammed the door. I realized then, with a knot in my stomach, how badly I had crushed her spirit.

At times I've wondered if I was part of the reason why she gave up wanting to be a missionary.

Although I may have been the one who took Bethany's dream from her in life, God enabled her *in death* to have a powerful story that truly is *going around the world*.

Through her memorial booklet, website and Spanish and Portuguese blogspots, Bethany has not only spread the gospel on this continent, but we have heard from others that her story has impacted lives abroad as well, including:

- Australia
- Brazil
- Canada
- China
- Columbia
- Dubai
- Great Britain
- Honduras
- India
- Mexico
- New Zealand
- Russia
- South Africa
- South Korea
- Venezuela

I pray Bethany's message of God's existence, mercy and love will continue to touch hearts. Believe it or not, mine was one of the first to be reached.

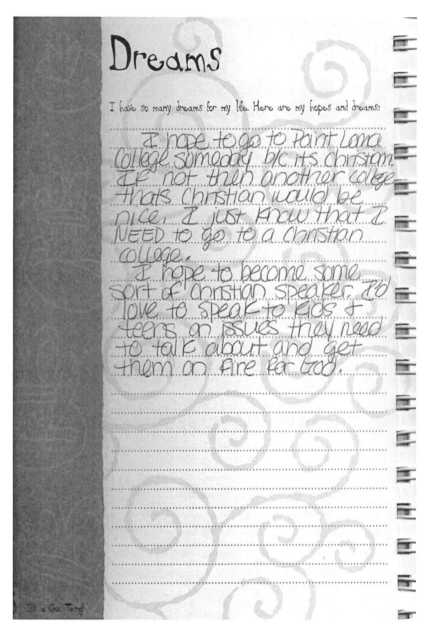

Dreams

I have so many dreams for my life. Here are my hopes and dreams:

I hope to go to Point Loma College someday b/c its christian. If not then another college thats christian would be nice. I just know that I NEED to go to a christian college.

I hope to become some sort of christian speaker. I'd love to speak to kids & teens on issues they need to talk about and get them on fire for God.

This is Bethany's last journal entry in the book *It's a God Thing*,[9] which was given to her by her grandparents, Richard & Evelyn Rivas, in June 2001.

Chapter 21:

Saved by Love

It is true that time heals, but often when I thought I had overcome my grief, something would happen to cause me to crumble again.

Thursday evening, April 5, 2007, I went to bed with a sense of peace and renewed hope. I had been writing steadily and was looking forward to the prospects of publishing this book.

Easter was approaching, but I did not dwell on it since holidays were always difficult to face after Bethany's death.

Although I seldom dreamt about her, I woke up that morning weeping uncontrollably, choking on tears.

Every detail in my dream had been so clear. I felt like I was *living* it.

It was Easter morning. I was standing at my closet, picking out a dress to wear, when my two daughters came bouncing into the room.

Kristin was about 7 and Bethany was about 9.

They were decked out in ruffles and lace, beaming with delight as they showed "Mommy" how they looked in their Easter finery.

Bethany and Kristin in dresses similar to that of Mom's dream.

As I turned to admire their dresses, I noticed Bethany had covered her face with a pale powder that made her look deathly white. A pang of agony pierced my heart.

Even though dreams sometimes feel real, there is usually a part that remains ethereal. In my dream, I knew Bethany was going to die at an early age.

Trying to control my trembling voice, I cupped her chin in my hand and looked down at her. "Are you Mommy's little ghost?" I asked.

I could not hide the tears filling my eyes. Bethany seemed oblivious to the white makeup. Instead, the same troubled look she had given me in the bathtub as a toddler now clouded her face.

I cannot account for her odd choice of words except to say that dreams must read our subconscious thoughts.

"What's wrong, Mommy?" she asked. "Has something come between us?"

I gathered her into my arms and held her tightly. "Yes, Bethany," I whispered, "*death* has come between us."

When I woke up, I still felt her hug around my neck and the warmth of her cheek against mine. My whole body shook as I sobbed with grief.

That morning, Clark and I took our daily walk on a local hiking trail. Yet, the vigor of the crisp morning air and the expectation of watching the sunrise held no joy for me.

My heart was still broken. I was aching with loneliness and longing for my daughter...for the little girl I had held so many times in my arms and whose cheek I had lovingly kissed.

No beauty in nature and no song of any bird could fill the emptiness.

I purposely chose upbeat music to listen to as I walked, hoping the songs would lift my spirits. Since my friend, Kenya, had given me Amy Grant's LIVE CD for Christmas, I popped it into my headphone set.

Even though the music was lively, my thoughts were sad and pensive. I wanted Bethany back!

Clark and I were nearing the end of the trail when the lyrics of the song "Saved by Love" caught my attention.

Amy Grant was singing that the love of her family kept her warm and nothing but death would leave her cold. Her words cut like a knife.

I thought curtly, "Well, I *have* experienced death, and it *has* left me cold." Then the next lines hit me even harder. She was saying even though life is sometimes lonely, it only makes her love Jesus more.

Suddenly, I heard Bethany's voice in my head, "MOM, LISTEN TO THESE WORDS!"

The lyrics continued. "I can't imagine ever leaving now. Now that I've been *saved by love*…."[8]

I could sense Bethany was sending me a beautiful message through the song. "Mom, God has turned my world around and I've been *saved by love!*"

Tears ran down my cheeks. The bitterness in my heart melted. I realized Bethany did not want to leave heaven.

Her life had been wild and tumultuous sometimes here on earth, but God had turned that all around.

She was safe. She was happy. She had been *saved by love.*

My mind searched for the date so I could remember this moment. *What day was it?*

I began to mentally calculate and then it struck me. It was April 6, 2007—*Good Friday*—the day we, as believers, celebrated Christ's ultimate sacrifice of love.

My heart rejoiced and burst within me!

Jesus died on this day over 2,000 years ago so Bethany could live...so *all of us* could live!

We can *all* be forgiven and receive His grace and mercy.

4Given

You, too, can be *saved by love*. It doesn't matter what you have done or what you are doing.

Christ came to set everyone free, and only His power can *truly* free us.

Whatever your addictions are, turn them over to Him. Whatever happened to you in the past, turn the pain, the anger and the memories over to Him.

If someone has wronged you or taken away something or someone you loved, give it to God. Let Him take the burden, and you will feel the weight lifted from your shoulders and your life.

If you want to be free, simply say this prayer and mean it from your heart. God will hear you.

"Heavenly Father, I am tired of struggling. I am tired of trying to handle life on my own. I know I have sinned and I am sorry. I repent and ask You to forgive me and set me free. I believe Christ died on the cross for me so I can have eternal life. Please come into my heart.

I receive the gift of the Holy Spirit to give me strength to overcome my addictions; to help me forgive others who have wronged me; and to stop doing the things I know are wrong. I love You and want to have a personal relationship with You. In Jesus' Name. Amen!"

If you said this prayer, you have now begun the amazing journey of having a personal relationship with Jesus Christ. He will begin to speak to you through your thoughts.

As you read the Bible and other Christian books and materials, there will be certain passages that will stand out and impress themselves on your consciousness.

They will speak to the very thing you have been wondering about. Or perhaps the sermons you hear will speak to your situation.

God will always find a way to meet your need if you seek Him. He will guide you to those who can help you, and He will give you strength to do what you need to do.

However, when you turn your life over to God, know that Satan will try hard to make you doubt God and yourself. He will also plague you with discouragement and tempt you to return to your old friends and habits.

After Bethany rededicated her life at a church summer camp in 2003, she wore a ring that said "4GIVEN" so the devil could not throw the past in her face.

She was on fire for God and felt He had called her into youth evangelism.

Yet, when we allowed her to hang around her old friends because she wanted to witness to them, she was pulled back into old habits. Soon, she became discouraged and gave up.

As a new Christian, the most beneficial thing you can do is find a group of believers who will nurture you as you begin your journey.

God directs us to do this in Hebrews 10:24-25 because He knows how vitally important it is for us to surround ourselves with others who will encourage us in the faith, and also love and support us.

If this book touched you in anyway, or if you accepted Jesus Christ into your life, I would love to hear from you. Please connect with me at sharonrivas.com.

If you are a Christian, I ask you to share this book with someone else who needs to know God is real.

If you are still undecided, I believe God is trying to reach you…and He will continue to do so until your last breath.

I hope you will eventually be one of those who meet my daughter in heaven and say, "Bethany, I am here because of *your story!*"

I eagerly expect and Hope that I will no way be ashamed, but will have sufficient courage so that now as always Christ will be exalted in my body, whether by life or by death.

For to me, to live is Christ and to die is gain.
*Phil. 1:20-21

Note discovered on the back of Bethany's bedroom door after she died.

Sermon #1

Bethany
Rivas

Do you really believe in God? Think about it. Are you absolutely sure that there's really a Divine power above us? What if the scientists are right? What if we really did just evolve from hairy animals?

IF you are someone out there that have ever doubted our God don't worry. It's perfectly natural because we are humans nothing more nothing less. Have you ever wondered how God can love us? I mean I'm sure you've heard "God loves you" from someone but have u ever wondered how they know that? I have asked all these questions myself. I used to not believe there was a God. I couldn't comprehend with my little feeble mind a God that I couldn't even see. One day someone asked me why your conscience doesn't feel bad when you do things for God. That really blew my mind. How come our conscience doesn't let us know that we're doing something wrong when we're doing it for God? Mine lets me know when I'm doing something wrong but not when I think about God and what I can do for Him. Now some of ya'll might be thinking that our minds are trained to be like that

Bethany's three-page, handwritten sermon found after her death.

but even when I was without God my conscience bothered me. Thank God my heart did not turn to stone before I found Jesus again. I looked at all the bad in the world and decided that a God wouldn't let all this bad stuff happen but without suffering no thankfulness could come. God has plans for everything and everyone just sometimes we don't understand them but when we get to Heaven u can ask God whatever u'd like. I used to not believe in ~~God~~ the Bible either. I just thought it was a book trying to get people to act a certain way. You might think the Bible is boring but it really isn't. If you really want to know about the man that split time, who claims to be ~~~~ God's son, then the Bible is a good place to start. Either Jesus was an extremly crazy man (like really just psycho) to be claiming and sacrificing what he did or there was some sort of truth he was saying. Do you think a man would suffer the worst death for a lie? If you had known him wouldn't you want to write something about Him? The people in the Bible were just like u & me they are just examples for us to learn from. I tell u

Continued on next page

the truth, if you dont believe in Jesus as the only way to our God then I hope youre right because if not you'll have all eternity to think about it. The Devil is no joke. He is quite real and he hates you and I, very much. In fact, he just cant wait for u to join him if you make the choice not to join Jesus. Just talk to God. If u want an answer be patient and keep the eyes of your heart open and if you'll seek God He will seek you. Remember the day you die is not the end but the begging-ing so pray hard and live loudly.

Epilogue

It was a cloudy afternoon in May 2007. As I washed my hands in the restroom of the Borders bookstore in Ocoee, FL, I might as well have been washing my hands of this entire book.

I was silently telling the Lord, "I quit! I don't have the energy or the desire to start over."

Apparently, He already knew what I was going to say. I had just met with Suzette, the editor of FarMor Publishing, to let her review the chapters I'd written.

I had worked hard on them, writing nonstop (literally) for 10 hours a day for over a week. My husband had prepared all the family meals and brought mine to me at the computer.

By the time I met Suzette at Borders, I was sick of writing, and I had *only* finished 10 chapters.

After reading the first few, she put them down and said sincerely, "Mrs. Rivas, you are a very good writer and you have an awesome story to tell, but I need you to start over."

I had begun my story with Bethany's birth and had planned to finish the book with her death. That seemed the appropriate way to tell a story.

However, Suzette wanted me to start with Bethany's death because that was where God's *miraculous interventions* had begun.

The request not only ruined my outline and invalidated my entire week of writing, but it also forced me to confront what I had been putting off.

To place myself emotionally back at the night Bethany died was something I had been dreading. I had been trying to work up to it gradually, buying time.

Now I would have to face it head on, beginning with the gut-wrenching pain of losing her.

Just being in Borders was hard. Bethany and I had met there so many times that I purposely avoided the bookstore. If a place could cause such pain, how could I stand reliving the night she died?

Suzette had quickly gathered her belongings and headed out for another appointment. I had slowly gathered my chapters and walked dejectedly to the restroom.

I stood at the sink and looked in the mirror. I had to face the truth. I couldn't do it. *I wouldn't do it.*

I walked slowly through the store, wondering how I would tell Suzette I was backing out. I decided to call her as soon as I got to the car.

When I reached the front door, I stepped aside to let a gentleman enter the store. As he passed by, a bolt of electricity went through me.

I turned around and watched him walk to a table of books near the front of the store. I stared at him, wondering if my eyes had deceived me.

For some reason, Zachery Tims of New Destiny Christian Center in Apopka, FL, looked a whole lot taller when he was on a platform preaching.

I walked around to his side as discreetly as possible and took another look. Without his suit on, I almost didn't recognize him.

"Excuse me, Sir," I said politely, "but are you Pastor Zachery Tims?"

He looked up and said pleasantly, "Yes."

I knew he was a busy man, but I just had to tell him how much his ministry meant to me. I thanked him for his television program and told him that my daughter had been killed two years ago.

During the months following her death, his messages had ministered to me over and over. I had always wanted to let him know, but I never thought I'd get the chance to do it in person.

He thanked me and then asked, "Do you mind if I ask how your daughter died?"

"It was a drunk-driving accident," I answered.

Remembering I had a memorial booklet in my bag, I pulled it out and gave it to him.

Then I mentioned that I had just met with an editor who had asked me to write a book about the many miracles surrounding Bethany's death...how God warned me that she was going to die...and how He answered my prayer and sent someone to pray with her before her death.

Pastor Tims was looking through the booklet as I spoke, and I told him he could keep it to read later. He thanked me, and I headed, once again, for the door.

I was on my way out when he called after me, "I'll be *anxious* to read it when you're done!"

Hesitantly, I stopped and turned around. I had a tenth of a second to decide how to respond.

Was I going to tell Pastor Tims that I had just given up and there would be *no* book?

For some reason I could not bring myself to tell him that I was quitting, not after all his sermons about overcoming obstacles and obeying God.

In a split second, I had to make a hard decision.

He was looking at me with so much sincerity and encouragement that I regained all the energy and motivation I had lost.

"Okay," I said, smiling.

As I walked to the car, I heard a voice softly say, "Sharon, I sent you Zachery Tims."

Suddenly, a lump sprang up in my throat and tears streamed down my face. It was God!

The voice continued gently, "I know this is hard. I know it's going to be a lot of work to start over. That's why I sent him. I knew he would be the only one who could get you to do it."

When I got in the car, I did call Suzette. I told her I would start over because I had promised Pastor Zachery Tims that I would finish my book.

We don't always know how our comments will affect people, but a word of encouragement may help them at the *exact* moment they need it.

I thank God for sending Pastor Tims to me that day.

Sadly, on August 12, 2011, only months after he was given preview chapters of this book, he passed away.

I am forever grateful to Pastor Zachery Tims for taking that *extra* moment to speak to me. It made this book possible.

You can learn more about Bethany on her mother's website
sharonrivas.com

To read her story in Spanish, go to
www.bethanyrivas-es.blogspot.com

To see the last video of Bethany
at her grandmother's birthday celebration,
go to YouTube.com and search for:
"Bethany Rivas Signs How Great Thou Art"

Mrs. Rivas is available to speak
at religious functions and as a representative for
Mothers Against Drunk Driving.

Thank you for your support!

God bless you,
The Rivas Family

References

1. *Angels Everywhere: Miracles & Messages* by Lynn Valentine. Copyright © 1999. This edition licensed to Hallmark Cards, Inc. by Premium Press America.

2. "Grace Like Rain" by Todd Agnew. Copyright © 2003. Ardent Records.

3. *Little Red Hen,* written/illustrated by Mrs. Floyd McCague. Copyright 1945, renewed 1968. Published and distributed by The Children's Bible Club, Milton, FL 32570. www.childrensbibleclub.com

4. *Born Again* by Charles W. Colson. Copyright © 2008. Chosen Books; *Against the Night: Living with the New Dark Ages* by Charles W. Colson, Copyright © 1999. Vine Books.

5. *Streams in the Desert: 366 Daily Devotional Readings* by L. B. Cowman. Copyright © 1997. Zondervan. Used by permission.

6. "Praise You in This Storm" by Casting Crowns. Bernie Herms/Mark Hall © 2005 Banahama Tunes (Admin. by Word Music, LLC), Word Music, LLC, Club Zoo Music, SWECS Music. All Rights Reserved. Used by permission.

7. National Highway Traffic Safety Administration www.nhtsa.gov.

8. "Saved By Love" by Amy Grant, Justin Peters and Chris Smith. "Lead Me On" album, 1988. A&M Records.

9. *It's a God Thing* by Karen Hill. Copyright © 2001. Thomas Nelson Inc.